Praise for *The Soul of E Business in the Knowledg*

"Imagine being personally mentored by two of the most insightful economic thinkers of our era to learn the most important lessons in modern business. *The Soul of Enterprise* book creates this reality. Baker and Kless share countless knowledge economy principles, in a simultaneously compelling and inspiring book."

— Matthew Burgess
Founder of knowledge economy law firm View Legal

"If you want to know the answers to questions like: How do I increase my return on equity? What's the secret to optimizing hours utilization? and What are the latest service industry best practices? This is not your book. But if you want to explore questions like: What's the purpose of business? Where does a company's value come from? and What ideas will define economic flourishing in the next hundred years? You've picked up the right text. In it, you'll be a fly on the wall as two of my mentors converse about the concepts they've mined and honed for years, and with which they've inspired many. But a word of caution, then a promise: Like Pandora's Box, these ideas are dangerous, and you will find it hard not to start changing the ways you do things. But if you do, you will also find a new satisfaction, as you re-ignite, *The Soul of Enterprise.* "

— Adrian Simmons
Chief Creative Designer, David G. Simmons, CPA

"I listen to every episode of my favorite podcast, *The Soul of Enterprise.* I am always deeply impressed by the profound and inspiring knowledge of economy and entrepreneurship Ron and Ed are sharing. To have this precious content condensed in this ebook is great."

— Markus Hartmann
CEO, axxios Consulting

"Remarkable! Ron Baker and Ed Kless share their deep knowledge and keen insight on how business should work."

— Robert E. Johnson
Chief Revenue Office, MECLABS

Except for this sentence this page was intentionally left blank.

The Soul of Enterprise
Dialogues on Business in the Knowledge Economy

Ronald J. Baker
Ed Kless

VeraSage Press
Petaluma, California

6/15

My dear
friend Joe,
Keep on
creating value.
Ed

To George Gilder

Thank you for opening my eyes, and mind, to the essential role of entrepreneurs in creating an economy full of wonder, wealth, surprise, and dynamism.

— RJB

To Christine

You are my soulmate, mo cushla! Thank you for being a partner with me in the ultimate entrepreneurial act — the bearing and raising of our children. Because of you and them I believe in a tomorrow that is better than today.

— EJK

Like a chrysalis, we're emerging from the economy of the Industrial Revolution — an economy confined to and limited by the Earth's physical resources—into, as one economist titled his book, "the economy in mind," in which there are no bounds on human imagination and the freedom to create is the most precious natural resource.

— President Ronald Reagan
Remarks at Moscow State University
May 31, 1988

Contents

Part 2 - The 'Effing' Debate: Efficiency vs. Effectiveness

Part 3 - A Theory of Everything

Part 4 - The Morality of Markets

Foreward

I know Ron and Ed quite well. They are dear friends, and they're incredibly insightful. So insightful, they asked an atheist to write the foreword to a book whose title refers to the soul. That's like asking a Mormon to write the foreword to *The Joy of Homebrewing*.

But please understand, I haven't read this book.

The main reason I haven't read it is because it's a modified transcript of Ron and Ed's VoiceAmerica radio shows. Conceptually, the format seems a little strange since I believe every chapter will be interrupted exactly three times with five commercials for Sage accounting products.

Since the book is a transcript of several conversations, it's a lot like a dialogue of Plato insofar as I haven't been able to finish reading a dialogue of Plato either. This book is also quite similar to the teachings of Socrates because by the time it's over you will willingly drink hemlock.

Ron is an expert on value pricing and economics. He's written the best-selling books *Pricing on Purpose*, *Professional's Guide to Value Pricing*, and *Implementing Value Pricing*. Although he's well aware of the law of diminishing returns, he's built a career on the assumption that his readers don't understand it. If you bought this book after reading *The Firm of the Future* and *Implementing Value Pricing*, you may also be interested in reading Amazon.com's return policy.

Ed is formally trained in theater and information systems. As both an actor and an early adopter of technology, it's no wonder Ed gravitated to the cutting-edge technology of radio.

Don't get me wrong. I tried to read this book. But I decided early on that I would take a drink every time either Ron or Ed said, "Yes," "Right," "Exactly," or "Absolutely," and I had alcohol poisoning by the middle of page six. (Editor's note: We even took some of these out of the transcripts and it is absurd.)

Despite all the sweet-talk above, please understand, I'm a *huge fan* of Ron and Ed.

Their depth of knowledge and insight into business and economics is profound. I've spent countless hours talking with them on the phone and in person. Not only do I never tire of their message, I find it helpful to regularly revisit their ideas. And every time I come back, I find new gems that were overlooked before, and they find new ways to challenge my thinking.

This book is sure to become an invaluable resource for us to transform our businesses as we access the brilliance that resides within the skulls of Ron Baker and Ed Kless.

Greg Kyte, CPA
Founder of Comedy CPE
www.ComedyCPE.com
G. Robert Newhart Non-Value Added Fellow
VeraSage Institute

Preface

How many a man has dated a new era in his life from the reading of a book.
— Henry David Thoreau

I gradually became aware of a chink in the armor of accounting in 1981, my sophomore year in college. I was studying to become a certified public accountant, believing it would allow me to do anything I wanted in the world of commerce since everyone kept telling me it was the language of business. I was being taught the importance of proper accounting in operating a successful enterprise, from the definition of profit to the necessity of cash flow. It was a body of knowledge, a tangible reality I could grasp, a prism in which the world of enterprise I so admired could be refracted so as to make sense to a naïve student who believed he knew more than he did.

One of the problems with education is the constant pursuit of practical knowledge at the expense of pursuing answers to profound questions. No doubt we all need practical knowledge to function in everyday life, earn a living, to just get by in the world. But I now realize people are not guided by what they *know*, but rather what they *believe* — their worldview, through which we all refract reality. And in August of 1981, my worldview was about to be punctured permanently, albeit quite gradually, indeed, imperceptibly at the time. Looking back, *Playboy* magazine may be most responsible.

No, not for the prurient reasons you are forgiven for immediately thinking of, but a far more banal explanation. As a barber, my father was an inveterate reader of *Playboy*'s interviews, which are excellent if you have ever bothered to read one with someone in whom you have an interest. The roster of interviewees is quite impressive — world leaders, politicians, writers, and so forth — some of whom, no doubt, are self conscious about appearing in such a publication. As a matter of fact, when devout Catholic William F. Buckley Jr. was asked why he would write for such a magazine, he wittily answered, "I write for *Playboy* because it is the fastest way to communicate with my 17-year-old son."

In any event, my father read the interview with George

Gilder in that August 1981 issue, which impressed him. Gilder had written *Wealth and Poverty*, a book Ronald Reagan was photographed with, along with giving it to members of his cabinet. Gilder would go on to become Ronald Reagan's most quoted living author. It is little remembered, but Reagan had a degree in economics from Eureka College, translating into a lifelong fascination with the writings of economic thinkers. For some reason, my father was impressed with the Gilder interview, explaining to me over lunch how this author had read over 200 books to write his, and was being hailed as the most articulate, albeit amateur, supply-side economist in the country.

Needless to say, I was not too impressed, pompously explaining to my dad how there are many crackpots who write economics books, most of which are useless, wrong, or belong in the fiction section of bookstores. I was mired in the mentality that only academic credentials lend credence to anyone writing on economics. Sure, Gilder may have been a graduate of Harvard, but he was not a professional economist such as Milton Friedman, whose book *Free to Choose* I had read the year before, which made a lasting impression on my worldview.

Fortunately for me, my father persisted, purchasing a copy of Gilder's book, convincingly insisting I should read it. I did. In one sitting. It changed my life. It opened my eyes to an entire new worldview that is beyond my capacity to describe in so brief a space. Little did I understand, but that was the sound of the first chink in the armor. The next chink came in 1982, when I read Warren T. Brookes's book, *The Economy in Mind*, the title of which you will see mentioned again in the Introduction, in a more historical setting.

The Soul of Enterprise brings me full circle to that first sitting of reading Gilder's penetrating insights. It is a journey that illuminates the opportunity cost of the accounting career I chose, which was the road not taken — that of the economist. I traded away, for the ability to capture and record the historical cost of everything, an understanding of the nature and origins of value, wealth, and poverty. It was not until later in my career, after I left the then — Big Eight accounting firm of KPMG that I understood this opportunity cost was increasingly becoming prohibitive.

I came to recognize I was ensconced in the accountant's worldview, a belief system and body of knowledge that cannot really explain how wealth is created — it can only record it after the fact. Accounting is not a theory, so it cannot help us peer into the future; it can only provide assurance on the past. It understands nothing but itself, since it is an identity equation. Worse, it leads businesspeople to believe they can only manage what they can measure, as if weighing ourselves more frequently will change our weight. It confuses cause and effect, and results with process. It can audit the drunk's bar bill, but cannot change or explain his behavior. Even more pernicious, it focuses businesspeople on solving problems and fretting over yesterday, rather than pursuing opportunities and creating our futures, resulting in a costly mediocrity.

I will always remember a conversation I was having over the audit of a genetic laboratory customer we had at KPMG, one that was working on a cure for AIDS. Of course, the losses in this start-up were as illustrious as the scientific credentials of its shareholders and board members. As we were poring over the balance sheet — bayoneting the wounded after the battle, as it were — I turned to my senior manager and said, "But you realize the most important assets of this company will never appear on its balance sheet, such as the intangibles of its employees and its entrepreneurial spirit." I didn't use the terms *intellectual* or *human capital* back then, since an accountant's world is divided neatly into tangible versus intangible. Nevertheless, the manager cocked his head, giving me one of those RCA Victrola dog looks, and said, "That's an excellent insight." I scored big points with that sagacity, impressing my superiors, but it was at the expense of my accounting worldview. Chink, crack. The armor was in scraps.

Thus began a passionate study of value, effectiveness, intellectual capital, along with the real source of profits, all represented in the knowledge economy this book expounds upon. The philosopher Heraclitus wrote, "You cannot step in the same river twice, because by the second step it will already have changed." Thus began my crossing of the river to reach the other side, seeing the world from a different direction — one of value, opportunity, and risk taking, rather than history, costs, problem solving, and an increasingly irrelevant accounting equation. I must say, this side of the river is more wondrous and panoramic, allowing me to explain with much greater clarity how the world really works. This is the only reason I write books — to help me explain the world I live in, while helping me think and constantly challenge my beliefs, subjecting them to the empirical test of reality.

It was not until the early 1990s that I began to fully comprehend that we had shifted from a service to a knowledge economy, comprised of knowledge workers who are different from industrial or service workers of a bygone era. They now comprise some 30 percent of the labor force (up from about 17 percent in 1950), but create the overwhelming majority of the value for most organizations. This is a lesson I am painfully reminded of every day, that my colleagues in professional knowledge firms have *still not learned*. They are walking around with an errant worldview, at a cost that is simply incalculable. If this book can challenge that worldview, even if only in the infinitesimal way relative to what Gilder's did to mine, it will have achieved its purpose.

To tie all these synchronous events together, bringing me full circle back to that first reading of Gilder's *Wealth and Poverty*, I was thunderstruck when I read the afterword to Gilder's book *Men and Marriage* in the early 1990s, titled "The Faith of Fathers." Gilder explains that he never knew his father, a bomber pilot who was killed in World War II. The day after Gilder received the first bound copies of his *Wealth and Poverty* manuscript, an uncle told him about a box he came across in his attic of some of his father's papers. Here is Gilder, explaining what he happened upon in those papers:

> I eagerly went through them; at the top was a 175-page manuscript on economics that he was working on when he died. One of its themes was the importance of what he called "intangible capital." It corresponded nearly perfectly with the key message of *Wealth and Poverty*: that the driving

force of a free economy was not material resources or even physical capital, but the metaphysical capital of family and faith. In fact, my father's work, if it had been completed, could very well have been entitled *Wealth and Poverty*.

Gilder goes on to explain the ultimate source of wealth, which is an outstanding inauguration to our journey together:

Demand, whether avaricious or just, is impotent to impel growth without disciplined, creative, and essentially moral producers of new value. All effective demand ultimately derives from supply; a society's income cannot exceed its output. The output of valuable goods depends not on lechery, prurience, lust, and license but on thrift, sacrifice, altruism, creativity, discipline, trust, and faith.

Greed, in fact, impels people to seek first their own comfort and security. The truly self-interested man most often turns to government to give him the benefits he lacked the moral discipline to earn on his own by serving others. ...Any system that does not uphold the value of freedom of individuals, however lowly, will miss most of the greatest technical and economic breakthroughs.

Then on Monday, June 10, 2013, George Gilder's latest book was published — *Knowledge and Power: The Information Theory of Capitalism and How It is Revolutionizing Our World* — and to my complete surprise and delight — he quoted from my book, *Mind Over Matter: Why Intellectual Capital is the Chief Source of Wealth*, published in 2008, which was inspired by Gilder's own *Wealth and Poverty* some 27 years earlier, and from which some of the material in this book has been adapted.

All because my father insisted I read a book.

I suppose all sons, at one time or another, come to appreciate the wisdom of Mark Twain: "When I was a boy of fourteen, my father was so ignorant I could hardly stand to have the old man around. But when I got to be twenty-one, I was astonished at how much he had learned." Thanks, Dad.

Peter Drucker, another mentor, was once asked why businesspeople fall for fads and fail to use empirical evidence, to which he replied: "Thinking is very hard work. And management fashions are a wonderful substitute for thinking." By and large, people do not engage in an endless search for the truth; they are busy trying to maximize utility, or *satisfice* — that is, do good enough. This book is written not so that you will think *like* us, but *with* us. But think you must, subjecting everything we say to your own belief system, challenging and discarding what you think is wrong, while acknowledging what may be right. Think of this book as a conversation between us; but you, dear reader, have the last word.

Ronald J. Baker
Petaluma, California
February 12, 2015

Ed Adds

Whereas Ron waxes poetic here, I will share a few practical concerns for the reader of this book.

First, as the primary editor, I am responsible for any and all errors and inconsistencies in the text. We consciously chose not to be overly concerned with form, erring instead on the side of providing the best possible substance. The careful reader will notice that sometimes terms are in a normal font, while sometimes they are either *italicized*, **bolded**, or even Capitalized. There is no particular cadence to this, other than at some point during the editing process I felt that it somehow aided the reader. If you find this distracting, I apologize.

Second, aside from blathering on during the actual recording of the show, my roles in the production of this book consisted of finding a transcription service, editing the commercials out of the audio files, and sending the transcribed files to Ron.

After he worked his magic on them, the files were returned to me for layout in our publishing software where I attempted to format them in an easily readable manner. In addition, I added hyperlinks to many (but not all) of the authors, books, and occasional concept that I felt some readers might wish to explore a bit further. Note that these links are rarely to such sites as wikipedia.com, but rather to sites that I feel will enhance your knowledge on the subject. Some of them are even a little fun. Happy Easter Egg hunting!

N.B. To the print version reader: The links are available in the Kindle version of this book and not the printed edition you have in your hands. This book was written as an ebook and the links appear in this printed edition, so you will know what you are missing. For the full experience, we suggest you go to http://verasage.com/dialogues

Third, we would love to hear from you about the book, the show or, frankly, anything else. Please feel free to email us at tsoe@verasage.com or tweet to #asktsoe.

Last, my wife Christine, who also assisted me in the editing process (but again, all short comings are mine), made an interesting comment as she labored over the manuscript. She said, "While Ron writes in em dashes, you (meaning me) speak in them." For this, I apologize, although as an admirer of Casey Stengel, who also famously spoke in parentheticals, I was a bit honored.

Another note on em dashes: We have opted to put spaces both before and after each one. This is nonstandard for publishing, but — as I am sure you will agree — make it much easier to highlight passages containing — especially beginning and ending with — them. (Editor's note: This is another ebook feature!)

Ed Kless
Allen, Texas
February 28, 2015

Ron's Acknowledgements

There is nothing like a dream to create the future.

— Victor Hugo, French poet, novelist, and playwright

This book is the physical embodiment of structural capital — one of the three types of intellectual capital it explores — but it is the product of an astounding collection of human and social capital. Once again, I have stood on the shoulders of giants, who have helped me see the world as it is and form my beliefs on why intellectual capital is the chief source of wealth.

Some of these giants have been absent teachers, educating me through their books. Most, though, I have had the great good fortune of meeting and working with. All deserve mention, all the while recognizing Reinhold Niebuhr's warning: "There is always some truth in the errors of others and some error in my truth." I, as always, accept the final responsibility for any and all errors that remain.

Untold gratitude must go to George Gilder for conducting an interview with *Playboy* that a barber read and was so inspired by, he purchased your book for his stubborn son, changing the boy's life forever after. Gilder has taught me mind over matter, mind over materialism, and mind over Marxism, with eloquence and logic without equal. His book *Wealth and Poverty* created the desire in me to write my own. His teachings on the morality of capitalism — especially his May 1997 speech to the Vatican, "The Soul of Silicon" — should be required reading for anyone who doubts the morality of free minds operating in free markets. Gilder is the Adam Smith of the twentieth and twenty-first centuries.

Many other economists have contributed to my understanding of intellectual capital: Warren T. Brookes, a former economics columnist for the *Boston Herald-American* and author of *The Economy in Mind*, a book that got me in trouble for being read at my desk — in a supposed knowledge organization — and the inspiration for the Introduction to this work. Former President Ronald Reagan, who cited Brookes' book in his speech at Moscow State University, has also contributed to my worldview. Many people forget that Reagan graduated from Eureka College with a degree in economics and was an inveterate reader of economic thinkers, including calling on Milton Friedman for counsel and distributing Gilder's *Wealth and Poverty* to his cabinet.

Friedrich Hayek, probably one of the most consequential economists and political philosophers of the twentieth century, was writing cogently about how markets capture, create, and disseminate knowledge in the most valuable manner long before anyone else. Hayek inspired Thomas Sowell, another economic genius, to write his seminal *Knowledge and Decisions*, which taught me why knowledge is critical to creating wealth.

Milton Friedman, RIP, along with Gilder, was my first introduction to economics, leaving an indelible impression on a young mind devoted to liberty. David Friedman (Milton's son), Steven Landsburg, Mark Skousen, and Deirdre McCloskey all taught me price theory, and professor McCloskey changed my worldview regarding the cause of the Industrial Revolution. Michael Novak, another of my favorite authors, has advanced the ethical argument that business enterprises are serious moral undertakings.

Of course, Peter Drucker, RIP, who introduced the terms *knowledge worker* and *knowledge economy* into the business lexicon over 55 years ago, has been a constant source of inspiration, teaching me the essentials of business without the fads, jargon, and unnecessary complexity of most business writers. Drucker had the rare gift of being simple while not being simplistic.

Karl Erik Sveiby is a pioneer in the area of intellectual capital, and the creator of the framework used in this work — breaking out intellectual capital into human, structural, and social. Thomas A. Stewart, a former writer for *Fortune* and editor of *Harvard Business Review*, also contributed to my thinking with his two fine books on the topic.

Even though I am not Jewish, I am proud to have my very own rabbi — Daniel Lapin. His grasp of human behavior is astounding, his book *Thou Shall Prosper* is profound, and he was the inspiration for the Epilogue to this work. Thank you, Rabbi.

In *The Structure of Scientific Revolutions*, Thomas Kuhn puts the question succinctly: "Suppose some well-trained young persons working in a discipline have a big idea in the nighttime; they propose a new interpretation of a problem that heretofore has defied resolution. How are they able, what must they do, to convert the entire profession ... to their way of seeing science and the world?" This is the very question my colleagues at VeraSage Institute ask themselves every single day, and while we may not have a definitive answer, we do know that change comes from influencing people one at a time. Another question we get asked, "Aren't you worried about people stealing your ideas?" This is probably the biggest lesson I've learned from working in the arena of ideas, and it comes from Howard Hathaway Aiken, who was a pioneer in computing, being the original conceptual designer behind IBM's Harvard Mark I computer: "Don't worry about people stealing your ideas. If your ideas are any good, you'll have to ram them down people's throats." A warm thank you to all my colleagues at VeraSage Institute: Mark Bailey, Justin Barnett, Kirk Bowman, Peter Byers, Mark Chinn, John Chisholm, Paul Dunn, Michelle Golden, Daryl Golemb, Brendon Harrex, Paul Kennedy, Ed Kless, Greg Kyte, Chris Marston, Tim McKey, Dan Morris, Paul O'Byrne (RIP), John Shaver, Jay Shepherd, Kurt Siemers, Adrian Simmons, Matthew Tol, and Tim Williams. I'm privileged to call all of you friends.

The entire team at the Professional Pricing Society deserves special thanks for continuing to put the discipline of pricing on the organizational charts in businesses around the world and for continuously supporting our work.

Another of my mentors was Sheila Kessler, RIP, who was a constant source of insights and wisdom regarding organizational functionality and dysfunctionality. I always learned so much from our exchanges, and I miss her immensely.

Thank you <u>Andrew Fyfe</u> for your brilliant and hilarious illustrations that decorate these pages, as well as the illustration we use for the Radio Show's logo. Your talent and wit *always* amazes and surprises me—you are a genius.

Much gratitude to Greg Kyte, G. Robert Newhart Non-value-added Fellow at VeraSage Institute, for writing the Foreword to this book, and brilliantly achieving what the humorist Mary Hirsch described: "Humor is a rubber sword — it allows you to make a point without drawing blood." Well, maybe you drew a little.

Ralph Waldo Emerson wrote in *Character*: "A chief event of life is the day in which we have encountered a mind that startled us." This aptly describes my colleague, Dan Morris, whose mind is like a thunderbolt — you never know when it is going to strike genius. Thank you, Dan, for constantly challenging the conventional wisdom and even some of my fervent beliefs.

When British chemist Michael Faraday was asked after a lecture if he meant to imply that a hated academic rival was always wrong, he snarled, "He's not that consistent." I'm sure this is how my British trusted adviser, Paul O'Byrne, RIP, would feel about some of the economic viewpoints expressed herein. Your spirit carries on within us every day.

C.G. Jung defines synchronicity as "a meaningful coincidence of two or more events, where something other than the probability of chance is involved." This describes my encounter with Robert Ciolino, who has indelibly changed my life. I've harbored a secret dream to be on the radio ever since I caught the bug by appearing on a radio talk show in Palm Springs back in 1996. Then Robert Ciolino called me in April of 2014. I'm proud to say Robert is the Executive Producer of our Radio Talk Show on Voice America Internet Radio. Robert has made my transition to radio as smooth as possible with his wisdom, guidance, humor, and continuous ideas on how to improve the show. He's always willing to go above and beyond the call of duty when we have questions, need help, or just want to brainstorm about the show, becoming a mentor to me in a short amount of time. I couldn't have asked for a better partner with whom to launch this new career. I cannot thank you enough, Robert. Dreams do come true.

The entire crew at Voice America has been a pleasure to work with, producing a remarkably professional product. A special shout out to our most frequent Voice America audio engineer, Matt Weidner, for keeping us on target and on time, all the while making it look easy (it's not).

Thanks to our sponsors for having faith in the future of a brand new show and our unique message on the soul of enterprise: Aimee Ertley and the entire team at Sage; Dan Kraus and the team at Leading Results; and Peter Wolf and the team at Azamba.

The American humorist Will Rogers once said, "A man only learns in two ways, one by reading, and the other by association with smarter people." There's much wisdom in this statement, as my ten-plus year corroboration with Ed Kless proves. I can't imagine doing the radio show without you. You are a constant inspiration, and one who likes to "dwell in/ Possibility," to borrow some verse from Emily Dickinson. I look forward to ever-expanding possibilities. Who says Libertarians and Conservatives can't get along? Thanks, Ed.

To Ed's lovely and gracious wife, Christine. Thanks for all your work on this book, and for keeping Ed humble.

Ambrose Bierce once wrote in a book review "The covers of this book are too far apart," a reaction I know my brother, Ken Baker, would undoubtedly agree with. Nevertheless, he remains an indefatigable supporter of my work and the best brother I could ever have asked for.

Anytime I receive an introduction that is far too generous, I am reminded of what President Lyndon Johnson used to say on similar occasions: "My father would have enjoyed it and my mother would have believed it." Fortunately for me, this is still — undeservedly — true, since my parents have been a constant source of encouragement and faith in my future.

Ed's Acknowledgements

*I've heard it said that people come into our lives for a reason,
bringing something we must learn and we are led to those who help us most
to grow, if we let them and we help them in return. Well, I don't know if I
believe that's true, but I know I'm who I am today because I knew you...*

*Like a comet pulled from orbit as it passes a sun, like a stream that
meets a boulder halfway through the wood; who can say if I've been changed
for the better? But because I knew you, I have been changed for good.*

— <u>For Good</u> from the Broadway musical *Wicked*, lyrics by
Stephen Schwartz

As Greg Kyte mentioned in the foreword, I have a background in the theatre, specifically musical theatre. At 11 I played Kurt in <u>The Sound of Music</u> in a church production. In my early twenties I played the title role in the Stephen Schwartz musical <u>Pippin</u>. I have been hooked on his work since then.

The lyric above from <u>Wicked</u> is the perfect explanation of why these acknowledgements will be lacking in some way. I believe that every person with whom we come into contact can be an influence on ours lives. Some people who are in our lives even for a brief period can influence what we think for decades. In some cases what they say or do only becomes clear to us much later — days, weeks, months, even years.

My mentor, Howard Hansen calls this phenomena "fuse lighting." So, to Howard and his partner Steve Geske, I thank you for lighting fuses for me. I am certain, I have only begun to feel the impact of some of those fuses.

In addition to performing since I was 11, I also minored in theatre in college. So, to Professor Ruis Woertendyke, and all my friends at College of White Plains — Pace University, for teaching this business major the power of using theatrical techniques in everyday work situations. I remember more from your classes and the plays we produced together than any of the business stuff.

The aforementioned production of *The Sound of Music* starred my father, Frank Kless as <u>Captain von Trapp</u>. During the run of the show, which was a mere two weeks long, he drove my mother in a driving snowstorm to the hospital where she delivered my youngest sister. He subsequently was admitted to the hospital a week later due to stomach ulcer. So, to my parents, Frank and Peggy Kless for their commitment to me for, literally, as long as I can remember. And, to my brother Rich, for being the most trusted critic I have of my work. And, to my sisters, Kristin and Eileen, for caring for my parents as they age and for always being able to tell me a mocking tale or jibe to please me.

After graduating from college, I began a most fascinating career as a consultant. With all the many things I have done and continue to do, when I am asked for my profession or title, my reply is always "Consultant." So, to the customers and business partners with whom I have worked over the past decades, for sharing their problems with me, allowing me to share my thoughts back, and creating new ideas which I hope have made your lives better. You have certainly made mine better.

While I still think of myself as consultant, I am fortunate to work at a place which has somehow allowed me to continue this work while weirdly working only for one company. So, to my colleagues at Sage, especially, Donald Deshaies, Joo Sohn, Diana Waterman, Jennifer Warawa, Aimee Ertley, and Greg Tirico, thank you for making my job, a joy. And, to former Sage colleagues Taylor Macdonald and Rob Johnson, for being mentors as well as friends.

My latest title is that of radio talk-show host. So, to our executive producer Robert Ciolino and engineer Matt Weidner for teaching us the ropes of the radio business and making us sound great each week. So, also, to our sponsors Dan Kraus of Leading Results and Peter Wolf of Azamba, truly without you, this book would not exist.

Of course, "host" is not exactly correct, as Ron and I "co-host" the show. He is too modest to admit that he bears the lion's share of the work since I work full-time for Sage, but he does and for that I truly thank him. In addition to being fun to work with, Ron is also a dear friend who has definitely changed me "for the better."

Although "Consultant" is the title I claim professionally, "Dad" is the title by which I am most honored. So, to Cailín, Sionáin, Éirinn, Sean, and Cara, thank you for teaching me the joy of fatherhood. I am sure I have made plenty of mistakes, but seeing each of you grow into the beautiful individuals that you are demonstrates that I made some good decisions too.

Of course, whether I am "Consultant" or "Dad" none of it would matter without my beautiful and brilliant wife, Christine, to whom this book and all my waking moments are dedicated. Thank you, for... well... EVERYTHING! "I have been changed for GOOD!"

About the Authors

Ronald J. Baker started his CPA career in 1984 with KPMG's Private Business Advisory Services in San Francisco. Today, he is the founder of VeraSage Institute — the leading think tank dedicated to educating professionals internationally-and a radio talk-show host on the VoiceAmerica show: *The Soul of Enterprise: Business in the Knowledge Economy*.

As a frequent speaker, writer, and educator, his work takes him around the world. He has been an instructor with the California CPA Education Foundation since 1995 and has authored 20 courses for them, including: *You Are What You Charge For: Success in Today's Emerging Experience Economy (with Daniel Morris); Alternatives to the Federal Income Tax; Trashing the Timesheet: A Declaration of Independence; Everyday Economics; Everyday Ethics: Doing Well by Doing Good; The Best Business Books You Should Read; Pricing on Purpose: Creating and Capturing Value; Measure What Matters to Customers*; and *Innovating Your Business Model*.

He is the author of six books, including: *Professional's Guide to Value Pricing; The Firm of the Future: A Guide for Accountants, Lawyers, and Other Professional Services*, co-authored with Paul Dunn; *Pricing on Purpose: Creating and Capturing Value; Measure What Matters to Customers: Using Key Predictive Indicators*; and *Mind Over Matter: Why Intellectual Capital is the Chief Source of Wealth*; and his latest book, *Implementing Value Pricing: A Radical Business Model for Professional Firms*.

Ron has toured the world, spreading his value pricing

message to over 120,000 professionals. He has been appointed to the American Institute of Certified Public Accountant's Group of One Hundred, a think tank of leaders to address the future of the profession; named on *Accounting Today's* 2001, 2002, 2003, 2004, 2005, 2006, 2007, 2011, 2012, 2013, and 2014 Top 100 Most Influential People in the profession; voted number six and nine of the Top Ten Most Influential People in the profession in 2012, 2013, and 2014; selected as one of LinkedIn's Influencer Bloggers; and received the 2003 Award for Instructor Excellence from the California CPA Education Foundation.

He graduated in 1984 from San Francisco State University, with a Bachelor of Science in accounting and a minor in economics. He is a graduate of Disney University and Cato University, and is a faculty member of the Professional Pricing Society. He presently resides in Petaluma, California.

To contact Ron Baker:
E-mail: Ron@verasage.com
Website/Blog: www.verasage.com
LinkedIn: http://linkd.in/SAG3IF
Twitter @ronaldbaker

Ed Kless joined Sage in July of 2003 and is currently the senior director of partner development and strategy. He develops and delivers curriculum for Sage business partners on the art and practice of small business consulting including the Sage Consulting Academy and Firm of the Future Symposium. He also facilitated the Sage Leadership Academy, a year-long program designed to assist Sage partners develop a continuous process of improvement in their organizations and serves as liaison to the Strategic Leadership Association.

Ed is also the cohost of the VoiceAmerica talk-show *The Soul of Enterprise: Business in the Knowledge Economy* with Ron Baker.

Prior to joining Sage, Ed worked with Tipping Point Advisors, an organization dedicated to the growth and development of software implementation partners. In 1996, he co-founded Third Wave Business Systems, a Microsoft Dynamics GP partner that grew to 20 team members and $5 million in revenue. At Third Wave, Ed developed the implementation methodology and led the CRM and ERP consulting teams.

Ed is a contributor to industry publications, including the *Journal of Accountancy, Harvard Business Review* and *HR.com,* and has spoken at many conferences worldwide on project management, pricing, and knowledge workers. He is also active in the Information Technology Alliance (ITA), Toastmasters, and is a senior fellow at the VeraSage Institute. He lives north of Dallas with his wife and two of his five children.

Currently he serves as chair of the Collin County Libertarian Party and ran for Texas State Senate, District 8 in

2010 and 2012.

To contact Ed Kless:
E-mail: Ed.Kless@VeraSage.com
Website/Blog: www.EdKless.com
LinkedIn: http://www.linkedin.com/in/edkless
Twitter @edkless

Introduction: Like a Chrysalis

We were among the last to understand that in the age of information science the most valuable asset is knowledge, springing from human imagination and creativity. We will be paying for our mistake for many years to come.

— Mikhail Gorbachev

Alvin and Heidi Toffler write in *Revolutionary Wealth* of the world's three wealth systems, "If the First Wave wealth system was chiefly based on growing things, and the Second Wave on making things, the Third Wave wealth system is increasingly based on serving, thinking, knowing, and experiencing." Iconically, these ages are represented by the plow, the assembly line, and the computer.

The transition from the Agrarian Age to the Industrial Age is conventionally dated from the late eighteenth to the early nineteenth century. The French employed the term *la révolution industrielle* (the Industrial Revolution) as early as the 1820s; Karl Marx used it in his writings in the mid-1800s, while historian Arnold Toynbee introduced the phrase to common parlance in the 1880s.

In the 1980s, it was popular to speak of the "Service Economy," given prominence by Karl Albrecht and Ron Zemke's book, *Service America*! In fact, the term service worker was coined around 1920, when fewer than half of all nonmanual workers were actually employed in service jobs — such as banking, insurance, restaurants, government, and so on. The terms knowledge industries, knowledge work, and knowledge worker are just a little more than half a century old. They were coined around 1959, simultaneously but independently, the first by a Princeton economist, Fritz Machlup, the second and third by Peter Drucker, in his book *The Landmarks of Tomorrow*.

Drucker later expanded on this new phenomenon in his 1968 book, *The Age of Discontinuity*. He posited it was the 1944 G.I.

31

Bill of Rights — which made available higher education to millions of veterans and was certainly the largest single investment in human capital up to that time–that helped cause the shift to a knowledge society.

Perhaps the term we use to describe this new economy is not up to us, just as the Industrial Revolution was not labeled by the people who launched that era. Echoing economist Joan Robinson's insistence that, "There is no advantage (and much error) in making definitions of words more precise than the subject matter they refer to," we remain uncomfortable with the terms knowledge economy and knowledge workers. The idea of a knowledge economy is a bit of an exaggeration since man cannot live on knowledge alone. Yet these definitions are distinguishing — and accurate — enough from prior ages that they will be used throughout this book.

Knowledge workers are not like workers from the Industrial Revolution, who were dependent on the employing organization's providing the means of production (factories and machines). Today, knowledge workers themselves own the firm's means of production in their heads. This is a seismic shift in our economy, the ramifications of which we are still trying to comprehend.

Any structural change in the economy is bound to cause severe dislocations as creative destruction undermines the existing industrial infrastructure. We witness the materialist fallacy rear its ugly head even today when politicians and pundits constantly ask if America can long sustain its present standard of living without a strong manufacturing base — the so-called "hamburger flipper" theory of low-paying service jobs. But this is precisely the wrong question. A better question would be to ask if a manufacturing base could long survive without a strong knowledge sector.

In fact, the distinction between goods and services is an anachronism, mostly used by governmental agencies. General Electric manufactures jet engines yet makes more money from servicing them. Is an Apple iPad merely a product or a service, or an experience — an escape from the mundane?

In an ironic twist on Karl Marx's idea of the proletarian revolution, in today's capitalist society, labor — what economists prefer to call human capital — trumps capital as the chief source of all wealth. British Prime Minister Tony Blair delivered a keynote speech at "Knowledge 2000: Conference on the Knowledge Driven Economy," where he stated:

I strongly believe that the knowledge economy is our best route for success and prosperity. But we must be careful not to make a fundamental mistake. We mustn't think that because the knowledge economy is the future, it will happen only in the future. The new knowledge economy is here, and it is now.

Twelve years prior to Blair's speech, another world leader stood before the icons of a materialist mind-set as an ambassador from the future, illuminating how the New Age economy, rooted in human creativity and imagination, would usher in a new era of prosperity for mankind.

The Ash Heap of History

Not since Richard Nixon had a president of the United States stood east of the Berlin Wall and spoken directly to the Soviet Union. Ronald Reagan, notorious for his virulent anticommunism, was certainly an improbable personality to address the citizens of the country he once described as an "evil empire." In an address to members of the British Parliament at the Palace of Westminster on June 8, 1982, Reagan prophetically predicted:

What I am describing now is a plan and a hope for the long term — the march of freedom and democracy which will leave Marxism-Leninism on the ash heap of history as it has left other tyrannies which stifle the freedom and muzzle the self-expression of the people.

Less than a year later, in his famous "evil empire" speech —

at the annual convention of the National Association of Evangelicals on March 8, 1983 — Reagan again envisaged communism's imminent implosion:

I believe that communism is another sad, bizarre chapter in human history whose last pages even now are being written. I believe this because the source of our strength in the quest for human freedom is not material, but spiritual. And because it knows no limitation, it must terrify and ultimately triumph over those who would enslave their fellow man.

Despite this rhetoric, and given the friendship that had developed between Reagan and Mikhail Gorbachev, the 1988 Moscow Summit was an opportunity for Reagan to speak directly to the future of the Soviet Union. According to Joshua Gilder, one of the speechwriters for the Moscow State University address, Reagan, "ever so nicely, explained that freedom and technology were going to leave the Soviets on the dust bin of history unless they changed their act — which of course they did, much sooner than we expected."

Here is how Reagan explained this rare opportunity in his memoirs, _An American Life_:

For more than thirty years, I'd been preaching about freedom and liberty. During my visit to Moscow, I was given a chance to do something I never dreamed I would do: Gorbachev let me lecture to some of the brightest young people of Moscow — among them some of the future leaders of the Soviet Union–about the blessings of democracy and individual freedom and free enterprise.

On what was for me an extraordinary day I never thought possible, I tried in a few minutes at Moscow State University to summarize a philosophy that had guided me most of my life.

There will be bumps in the road. But after talking with these bright young people in Moscow and seeing what was happening in their country, I couldn't help but feel optimistic: We were at the threshold of a new era in the political and economic history of the world.

I can't wait to see where it will lead us.

Here is how Reagan set the stage in his book, *Speaking My Mind*:

The trip to Moscow was one of the most intriguing experiences of my years in office. You can understand more about a place by just seeing it. One thing I noticed was that there is such a visible break in the history of the Russian people. It's right there in the architecture.

The architecture of Moscow State University is quite ominous. The university is housed in this threatening, yes, evil-looking, building erected by Stalin. But speaking to these students, I felt I could have been speaking to students anywhere. The coldness disappeared.

What a step forward it was just being there in that auditorium with the big bust of Lenin right behind me. I couldn't speak to the entire student body because the hall wasn't large enough, so the Soviets only let in students who were members of the Young Communist League. I didn't know that at the time, but it didn't seem to make any difference because I could feel that I was still getting a good reaction. I could see the students turn to each other and nod every once in a while, occasionally smile. I came away from there with a very good feeling.

Ed and I love this speech, believing it to be one of the best Ronald Reagan ever delivered. We play a part of it to open our radio show, the same section that is the epigraph to this book. You can watch the entire speech here, but we have also reproduced it in its entirety in the Supplemental Material at the end of this chapter. It perfectly encapsulates the spirit of our message on *The Soul of*

Enterprise: Business in the Knowledge Economy.

Creative Destruction

There is perhaps no better living proof of Reagan's message than a Finnish-born fanatical computer programmer who at the age of 20 posted an e-mail on a Newsgroup, which began, "I'm doing a (free) operating system." In a twist of irony, this youngster's father, Nil Torvalds, was active in the Communist party since he was a student in college during the 1960s, of which he later admitted "his enthusiasm for communism may have been born of naiveté."

Nil's son, Linus Torvalds, developed the Linux operating system as a graduate student at the University of Helsinki, the largest collaborative project in the history of the world, made possible by the very revolution then taking place that Reagan had described in his speech.

Today, approximately 40 percent of American companies use the Linux operating system, along with more than 160 governments. Both Linus and Bill Gates created enormous wealth, yet both required only a modicum of capital; while the latter used a corporation, the former did not. Both relied on intellectual capital, the source of all wealth.

Reagan used the metaphor of a chrysalis to describe how the world economy was shifting from the Industrial Revolution to the Information Era — what we are calling the knowledge or intellectual capital economy — even giving a nod to the subjective theory of value by describing how the value of a silicon chip lies not "in the sand from which it is made, but in the microscopic architecture designed into it by ingenious human minds."

Think of the wealth Intel has created since its beginnings in 1968, largely from products made by one of nature's most abundant resources — sand. If a farmer in Palo Alto, California, had been told in 1900 that in less than 100 years' time only 2 percent of the population would be farmers, as opposed to a majority of workers at that time, he would have thought the Valley to be a desert wasteland rather than the innovative and creative fount of technology it has become. Even Detroit now spends more on silicon chips than it does on steel for its automobiles, another illustration of the triumph of mind over matter.

The chrysalis metaphor sounds romantic, but the transformation is anything but romantic for the caterpillar, which loses its legs and its sight, and whose very body is torn apart until it emerges with its splendid wings. Likewise, when economies shift from one era into another, there are the inevitable dislocations, adjustments, and creative destruction that take place to the existing infrastructure.

This very process is still unfolding in the former Soviet Union. Many books have been published since Karl Marx's day on — what he believed — was the inexorable transition from capitalism to communism. Very few books have been written on the actual alteration from communism to capitalism taking place around the world. One pundit cracked that the transition from communism to capitalism was alcoholism.

Consider the predicament of Mikhail Gorbachev when he took over the former Soviet Union. Here was a man whose entire world paradigm of communism was literally swept onto the ash heap of history, as Reagan had stated. He immediately blamed his predecessors for all his problems. In fact, a running joke in the Soviet Union at the time went something like this:

A new manager of a collective farm finds two letters from his predecessor, with instructions to open the first when difficulties begin. When the farm fails to meet its quotas, the manager opens the first letter, which says, "Blame me." He does. It buys some time. But the farm fails again and he comes under fresh criticism, so he opens the second letter. It says: "Prepare two letters."

It is time for leaders in the business community to stop emulating their predecessors blindly and instead embrace the opportunities of the knowledge economy. This transition will take an enormous amount of faith in the future; an unleashing of the human spirit; the recognition of the universal desire for freedom; and the creativity of the ordinary person to perform extraordinary acts of wealth creation and contribute to something larger than themselves. It requires a country, or a company, to forget about yesterday and begin creating tomorrow.

Throughout history, the "physical fallacy" was an idea that reigned supreme. Economists now have a far better understanding of how wealth is created from free minds operating in free markets. This can be seen by observing various developing economies escaping the shackles of poverty, creating wealth and a better standard of living for their populations.

It is now clear that approximately 80 percent of the wealth-creating capacity of a country resides in human capital, and economists have proven this at the macro level of economic organization. What is needed now is to apply these same ideas at the micro level of the business entity by positing new theories for the knowledge company of the future. Let us begin.

Supplemental Material

President Ronald Reagan
Remarks at Moscow State University, May 31, 1988

Thank you, Rector Logunov, and I want to thank all of you very much for a very warm welcome. It's a great pleasure to be here at Moscow State University, and I want to thank you all for turning out. I know you must be very busy this week, studying and taking your final examinations. So, let me just say zhelayu vam uspekha [I wish you success]. Nancy couldn't make it today because she's visiting Leningrad, which she tells me is a very beautiful city, but she, too, says hello and wishes you all good luck.

Let me say it's also a great pleasure to once again have this opportunity to speak directly to the people of the Soviet Union. Before I left Washington, I received many heartfelt letters and telegrams asking me to carry here a simple message, perhaps, but also some of the most important business of this summit: It is a message of peace and good will and hope for a growing friendship and closeness between our two peoples.

As you know, I've come to Moscow to meet with one of your most distinguished graduates. In this, our fourth summit, General Secretary Gorbachev and I have spent many hours together, and I feel that we're getting to know each other well. Our discussions, of course, have been focused primarily on many of the important issues of the day, issues I want to touch on with you in a few moments. But first I want to take a little time to talk to you much as I would to any group of university students in the United States. I want to talk not just of the realities of today but of the possibilities of tomorrow.

Standing here before a mural of your revolution, I want to talk about a very different revolution that is taking place right now, quietly sweeping the globe without bloodshed or conflict. Its effects are peaceful, but they will fundamentally alter our world, shatter old assumptions, and reshape our lives. It's easy to underestimate because it's not accompanied by banners or fanfare. It's been called the technological or information revolution, and as its emblem, one might take the tiny silicon chip, no bigger than a fingerprint. One of these chips has more computing power than a roomful of old-style computers.

As part of an exchange program, we now have an exhibition touring your country that shows how information technology is transforming our lives — replacing manual labor with robots, forecasting weather for farmers, or mapping the genetic code of DNA for medical researchers. These microcomputers today aid the design of everything from houses to cars to spacecraft; they even design better and faster computers. They can translate English into Russian or enable the blind to read or help Michael Jackson produce on one synthesizer the sounds of a whole orchestra. Linked by a network of satellites and fiber-optic cables, one individual with a desktop computer and a telephone commands resources unavailable to the largest governments just a few years ago.

Like a chrysalis, we're emerging from the economy of the

Industrial Revolution — an economy confined to and limited by the Earth's physical resources — into, as one economist titled his book, "the economy in mind," in which there are no bounds on human imagination and the freedom to create is the most precious natural resource. Think of that little computer chip. Its value isn't in the sand from which it is made but in the microscopic architecture designed into it by ingenious human minds. Or take the example of the satellite relaying this broadcast around the world, which replaces thousands of tons of copper mined from the Earth and molded into wire. In the new economy, human invention increasingly makes physical resources obsolete. We're breaking through the material conditions of existence to a world where man creates his own destiny. Even as we explore the most advanced reaches of science, we're returning to the age-old wisdom of our culture, a wisdom contained in the book of Genesis in the Bible: In the beginning was the spirit, and it was from this spirit that the material abundance of creation issued forth.

But progress is not foreordained. The key is freedom — freedom of thought, freedom of information, freedom of communication. The renowned scientist, scholar, and founding father of this university, Mikhail Lomonosov, knew that. "It is common knowledge," he said, "that the achievements of science are considerable and rapid, particularly once the yoke of slavery is cast off and replaced by the freedom of philosophy." You know, one of the first contacts between your country and mine took place between Russian and American explorers. The Americans were members of Cook's last voyage on an expedition searching for an Arctic passage; on the island of Unalaska, they came upon the Russians, who took them in, and together with the native inhabitants, held a prayer service on the ice.

The explorers of the modern era are the entrepreneurs, men with vision, with the courage to take risks and faith enough to brave the unknown. These entrepreneurs and their small enterprises are responsible for almost all the economic growth in the United States. They are the prime movers of the technological revolution. In fact, one of the largest personal computer firms in the United States was started by two college students, no older than you, in the garage behind their home. Some people, even in

40

my own country, look at the riot of experiment that is the free market and see only waste. What of all the entrepreneurs that fail? Well, many do, particularly the successful ones; often several times. And if you ask them the secret of their success, they'll tell you it's all that they learned in their struggles along the way; yes, it's what they learned from failing. Like an athlete in competition or a scholar in pursuit of the truth, experience is the greatest teacher.

And that's why it's so hard for government planners, no matter how sophisticated, to ever substitute for millions of individuals working night and day to make their dreams come true. The fact is, bureaucracies are a problem around the world. There's an old story about a town — it could be anywhere — with a bureaucrat who is known to be a good-for-nothing, but he somehow had always hung on to power. So one day, in a town meeting, an old woman got up and said to him: "There is a folk legend here where I come from that when a baby is born, an angel comes down from heaven and kisses it on one part of its body. If the angel kisses him on his hand, he becomes a handyman. If he kisses him on his forehead, he becomes bright and clever. And I've been trying to figure out where the angel kissed you so that you should sit there for so long and do nothing." [Laughter]

We are seeing the power of economic freedom spreading around the world. Places such as the Republic of Korea, Singapore, Taiwan have vaulted into the technological era, barely pausing in the industrial age along the way. Low-tax agricultural policies in the subcontinent mean that in some years India is now a net exporter of food. Perhaps most exciting are the winds of change that are blowing over the People's Republic of China, where one-quarter of the world's population is now getting its first taste of economic freedom. At the same time, the growth of democracy has become one of the most powerful political movements of our age. In Latin America in the 1970s, only a third of the population lived under democratic government; today over 90 percent does. In the Philippines, in the Republic of Korea, free, contested, democratic elections are the order of the day. Throughout the world, free markets are the model for growth. Democracy is the standard by which governments are measured.

We Americans make no secret of our belief in freedom. In fact, it's something of a national pastime. Every 4 years the American people choose a new President, and 1988 is one of those years. At one point there were 13 major candidates running in the two major parties, not to mention all the others, including the Socialist and Libertarian candidates — all trying to get my job. About 1,000 local television stations, 8,500 radio stations, and 1,700 daily newspapers—each one an independent, private enterprise, fiercely independent of the Government — report on the candidates, grill them in interviews, and bring them together for debates. In the end, the people vote; they decide who will be the next President. But freedom doesn't begin or end with elections.

Go to any American town, to take just an example, and you'll see dozens of churches, representing many different beliefs — in many places, synagogues and mosques — and you'll see families of every conceivable nationality worshiping together. Go into any schoolroom, and there you will see children being taught the Declaration of Independence, that they are endowed by their Creator with certain unalienable rights — among them life, liberty, and the pursuit of happiness — that no government can justly deny; the guarantees in their Constitution for freedom of speech, freedom of assembly, and freedom of religion. Go into any courtroom, and there will preside an independent judge, beholden to no government power. There every defendant has the right to a trial by a jury of his peers, usually 12 men and women — common citizens; they are the ones, the only ones, who weigh the evidence and decide on guilt or innocence. In that court, the accused is innocent until proven guilty, and the word of a policeman or any official has no greater legal standing than the word of the accused. Go to any university campus, and there you'll find an open, sometimes heated discussion of the problems in American society and what can be done to correct them. Turn on the television, and you'll see the legislature conducting the business of government right there before the camera, debating and voting on the legislation that will become the law of the land. March in any demonstration, and there are many of them; the people's right of assembly is guaranteed in the Constitution and protected by the police. Go into any union hall, where the members know their right to strike is protected by law. As a matter of fact, one of the many jobs I had before this one was being president of a union, the Screen Actors Guild. I led my union out on strike, and I'm proud to say we won.

But freedom is more even than this. Freedom is the right to question and change the established way of doing things. It is the continuing revolution of the marketplace. It is the understanding that allows us to recognize shortcomings and seek solutions. It is the right to put forth an idea, scoffed at by the experts, and watch it catch fire among the people. It is the right to dream — to follow your dream or stick to your conscience, even if you're the only one in a sea of doubters. Freedom is the recognition that no single person, no single authority or government has a monopoly on the truth, but that every individual life is infinitely precious, that every one of us put on this world has been put there for a reason and has something to offer.

America is a nation made up of hundreds of nationalities. Our ties to you are more than ones of good feeling; they're ties of kinship. In America, you'll find Russians, Armenians, Ukrainians, peoples from Eastern Europe and Central Asia. They come from every part of this vast continent, from every continent, to live in harmony, seeking a place where each cultural heritage is respected, each is valued for its diverse strengths and beauties and the richness it brings to our lives. Recently, a few individuals and families have been allowed to visit relatives in the West. We can only hope that it won't be long before all are allowed to do so and Ukrainian-Americans, Baltic-Americans, Armenian-Americans can freely visit their homelands, just as this Irish-American visits his.

Freedom, it has been said, makes people selfish and materialistic, but Americans are one of the most religious peoples on Earth. Because they know that liberty, just as life itself, is not earned but a gift from God, they seek to share that gift with the world. "Reason and experience," said George Washington in his Farewell Address, "both forbid us to expect that national morality can prevail in exclusion of religious principle. And it is substantially true, that virtue or morality is a necessary spring of popular government." Democracy is less a system of government than it is a system to keep government limited, unintrusive; a system of constraints on power to keep politics and government secondary to the important things in life, the true sources of value found only in family and faith.

But I hope you know I go on about these things not simply to extol the virtues of my own country but to speak to the true greatness of the heart and soul of your land. Who, after all, needs to tell the land of Dostoyevski about the quest for truth, the home of Kandinski and Scriabin about imagination, the rich and noble culture of the Uzbek man of letters Alisher Navoi about beauty and heart? The great culture of your diverse land speaks with a glowing passion to all humanity. Let me cite one of the most eloquent contemporary passages on human freedom. It comes, not from the literature of America, but from this country, from one of the greatest writers of the 20th century, Boris Pasternak, in the novel Dr. Zhivago. He writes: "I think that if the beast who sleeps in man could be held down by threats—any kind of threat, whether of jail or of retribution after death — then the highest emblem of humanity would be the lion tamer in the circus with his whip, not the prophet who sacrificed himself. But this is just the point — what has for centuries raised man above the beast is not the cudgel, but an inward music — the irresistible power of unarmed truth."

The irresistible power of unarmed truth. Today the world looks expectantly to signs of change, steps toward greater freedom in the Soviet Union. We watch and we hope as we see positive changes taking place. There are some, I know, in your society who fear that change will bring only disruption and discontinuity, who fear to embrace the hope of the future — sometimes it takes faith. It's like that scene in the cowboy movie Butch Cassidy and the Sundance Kid, which some here in Moscow recently had a chance to see. The posse is closing in on the two outlaws, Butch and Sundance, who find themselves trapped on the edge of a cliff, with a sheer drop of hundreds of feet to the raging rapids below. Butch turns to Sundance and says their only hope is to jump into the river below, but Sundance refuses. He says he'd rather fight it out with the posse, even though they're hopelessly outnumbered. Butch says that's suicide and urges him to jump, but Sundance still refuses and finally admits, "I can't swim." Butch breaks up laughing and says, "You crazy fool, the fall will probably kill you." And, by the way, both Butch and Sundance made it, in case you didn't see the movie. I think what I've just been talking about is perestroika and what its goals are.

But change would not mean rejection of the past. Like a tree growing strong through the seasons, rooted in the Earth and drawing life from the Sun, so, too, positive change must be rooted in traditional values— in the land, in culture, in family and community — and it must take its life from the eternal things, from the source of all life, which is faith. Such change will lead to new understandings, new opportunities, to a broader future in which the tradition is not supplanted but finds its full flowering. That is the future beckoning to your generation.

At the same time, we should remember that reform that is not institutionalized will always be insecure. Such freedom will always be looking over its shoulder. A bird on a tether, no matter how long the rope, can always be pulled back. And that is why, in my conversation with General Secretary Gorbachev, I have spoken of how important it is to institutionalize change — to put guarantees on reform. And we've been talking together about one sad reminder of a divided world: the Berlin Wall. It's time to remove the barriers that keep people apart.

I'm proposing an increased exchange program of high school students between our countries. General Secretary Gorbachev mentioned on Sunday a wonderful phrase you have in Russian for this: "Better to see something once than to hear about it a hundred times." Mr. Gorbachev and I first began working on this in 1985. In our discussion today, we agreed on working up to several thousand exchanges a year from each country in the near future. But not everyone can travel across the continents and oceans. Words travel lighter, and that's why we'd like to make available to this country more of our 11,000 magazines and periodicals and our television and radio shows that can be beamed off a satellite in seconds. Nothing would please us more than for the Soviet people to get to know us better and to understand our way of life.

Just a few years ago, few would have imagined the progress our two nations have made together. The INF treaty, which General Secretary Gorbachev and I signed last December in Washington and whose instruments of ratification we will exchange tomorrow — the first true nuclear arms reduction treaty in history, calling for the elimination of an entire class of U.S. and Soviet nuclear missiles. And just 16 days ago, we saw the beginning of your withdrawal from Afghanistan, which gives us hope that soon the fighting may end and the healing may begin and that that suffering country may find self-determination, unity, and peace at long last.

It's my fervent hope that our constructive cooperation on these issues will be carried on to address the continuing destruction and conflicts in many regions of the globe and that the serious discussions that led to the Geneva accords on Afghanistan will help lead to solutions in southern Africa, Ethiopia, Cambodia, the Persian Gulf, and Central America. I have often said: Nations do not distrust each other because they are armed; they are armed because they distrust each other. If this globe is to live in peace and prosper, if it is to embrace all the possibilities of the technological revolution, then nations must renounce, once and for all, the right to an expansionist foreign policy. Peace between nations must be an enduring goal, not a tactical stage in a continuing conflict.

I've been told that there's a popular song in your country — perhaps you know it — whose evocative refrain asks the question, "Do the Russians want a war?" In answer it says: "Go ask that silence lingering in the air, above the birch and poplar there; beneath those trees the soldiers lie. Go ask my mother, ask my wife; then you will have to ask no more, 'Do the Russians want a war?'" But what of your one-time allies? What of those who embraced you on the Elbe? What if we were to ask the watery graves of the Pacific or the European battlefields where America's fallen were buried far from home? What if we were to ask their mothers, sisters, and sons, do Americans want war? Ask us, too, and you'll find the same answer, the same longing in every heart.

People do not make wars; governments do. And no mother would ever willingly sacrifice her sons for territorial gain, for economic advantage, for ideology. A people free to choose will always choose peace.

Americans seek always to make friends of old antagonists. After a colonial revolution with Britain, we have cemented for all ages the ties of kinship between our nations. After a terrible Civil War between North and South, we healed our wounds and found true unity as a nation. We fought two world wars in my lifetime against Germany and one with Japan, but now the Federal Republic of Germany and Japan are two of our closest allies and friends.

Some people point to the trade disputes between us as a sign of strain, but they're the frictions of all families, and the family of free nations is a big and vital and sometimes boisterous one. I can tell you that nothing would please my heart more than in my lifetime to see American and Soviet diplomats grappling with the problem of trade disputes between America and a growing, exuberant, exporting Soviet Union that had opened up to economic freedom and growth.

And as important as these official people-to-people exchanges are, nothing would please me more than for them to become unnecessary, to see travel between East and West become so routine that university students in the Soviet Union could take a month off in the summer and, just like students in the West do now, put packs on their backs and travel from country to country in Europe with barely a passport check in between. Nothing would please me more than to see the day that a concert promoter in, say, England could call up a Soviet rock group, without going through any government agency, and have them playing in Liverpool the next night. Is this just a dream? Perhaps, but it is a dream that is our responsibility to have come true.

Your generation is living in one of the most exciting, hopeful times in Soviet history. It is a time when the first breath of freedom stirs the air and the heart beats to the accelerated rhythm of hope, when the accumulated spiritual energies of a long silence yearn to break free. I am reminded of the famous passage near the end of Gogol's Dead Souls. Comparing his nation to a speeding troika, Gogol asks what will be its destination. But he writes, "There was no answer save the bell pouring forth marvelous sound."

We do not know what the conclusion will be of this journey, but we're hopeful that the promise of reform will be fulfilled. In this Moscow spring, this May 1988, we may be allowed that hope: that freedom, like the fresh green sapling planted over Tolstoy's grave, will blossom forth at last in the rich fertile soil of your people and culture. We may be allowed to hope that the marvelous sound of a new openness will keep rising through, ringing through, leading to a new world of reconciliation, friendship, and peace.

Thank you all very much, and da blagoslovit vas gospod — God bless you.

Part 1 — The Knowledge Economy

Chapter 1: <u>The Economy in Mind</u>

We know that the source of wealth is something specifically human: knowledge. If we apply knowledge to tasks that we already know how to do, we call it productivity. If we apply knowledge to tasks that are new and different, we call it innovation. Only knowledge allows us to achieve these two goals.

— Peter Drucker

Ron: Ed, I have a question for you.

Ed: Fire away, sir.

Ron: How much does the economy weigh?

Ed: There's got to be a lot of trans fats in the economy, so I'm thinking it weighs lots.

Ron: I didn't mean people. We know they've gotten heavier over time. How much do you think the economy weighs today compared to 1950? By the way, this was a question that <u>Alan Greenspan</u> used to pose to audiences to completely stump them.

Ed: Yeah, I really have no idea how much the economy weighs, no clue.

Ron: Would you guess heavier, lighter, or the same?

Ed: If you're comparing today to 1950, it's got to be heavier.

Ron: When I first read this, that's exactly what I thought. Greenspan just gave one example of the SKUs, the <u>Stock Keeping Units</u>, of just New York City being 10 to the 10th power. The answer is that it weighs the same. Even though the economy's output compared to today — or even at the time that Greenspan asked this, which was the early 2000s — is roughly seven times more than the output in real dollars than it was in 1950, and yet it weighs the same.

Ed: Wow! Okay, so you're talking about because now a book isn't a book; it's a Kindle, and music on MP3 players, etc. Alright, this is starting to make sense now if you switch to digital.

Ron: Right, if you compare atoms to bits, the atom being the physical world and the bits being the digital world. We can put an entire library on a little nano iPad; compare that to a jukebox, or think about your old record or CD collection; or all the newspapers that used to be delivered on everybody's doorstep, and now you just go online and read them, and like you said, books.

I found that to be very interesting, but it illustrates that the real economy is in mind. It's not in physical things. It's in our minds and that's really the point.

Ed: Hence, the title of this chapter, The Economy in Mind.

Ron: Thomas Sowell is one of my favorite all-time economists. He's a fantastic historian of economic ideas and he wrote a great book in 1996 called *Knowledge and Decisions*, where he wrote, "After all, the caveman had the same natural resources at their disposal as we have today, and the difference between their standard of living and ours is a difference between the knowledge they could bring to bear on those resources and the knowledge used today."

What an epiphany and an interesting way to think about it. The caveman had oil, but he didn't have a combustion engine. What created the combustion engine was man's creativity, imagination, and knowledge.

Ed: Yeah. I guess up until the late 1800s, oil was a problem to be dealt with. It came up through the fields and the guck; we need to get rid of the guck.

Ron: It was a nuisance. If you were a farmer, you didn't know what to do with this guck. Like we say, if we ever find a replacement for oil, its value is going to go back to zero. We used to use whale oil until Rockefeller saved the whales. You won't see Greenpeace giving him any credit for it, but he certainly did.

Ed: No, absolutely. If you go back to your example of New York City, my hometown, the reason why all of the homes in Manhattan are up on a stoop is to get over the smell from the horse dung.

Ron: That's right. If you just take a broad sweep of history real quick, obviously, we were a hunter-gatherer economy at one point, and then we transformed into an agrarian economy, and then of course, we had the Industrial Revolution and then some time around the 1920s we became a service economy.

In 1959, Peter Drucker, along with another economist, Fritz Machlup, identified a trend that was happening and they actually both coined the term, separately, the "knowledge economy," and of course, that's the subtitle of our radio show, *Business in the Knowledge Economy*, so we wanted to take some time to explain what exactly that means and how profound and tectonic a shift it is.

Ed: Going back to your example of the stages of society, what was the carbon footprint of early man? When you have a hunter-gatherer society, with the amount of land that you need in order to sustain a small population, it's just enormous. It wasn't until man tamed the surroundings and became an agrarian, and more sedentary, society that the footprint was reduced.

Data, Information and Knowledge

Ron: Sometimes you hear how we're in an information economy, which goes back to Stewart Brand, who was the founder of the *Whole Earth Catalog*; he's an icon out here in California. His famous line, "Information wants to be free," and we certainly see that on the web today. However, there's a big difference between information and knowledge.

Ed: A huge difference. In fact, I extrapolated this from Peter Drucker. Think of a pyramid, at the base of this pyramid is data.

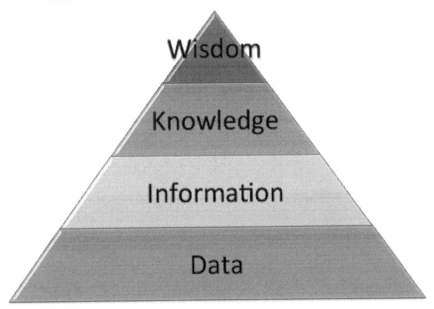

All companies have data, lots and lots of data. Before computers, this data existed on index cards and paper throughout the system. They all had this data and then on top of the data, we then have information. That information is really a subset of the data, and any kind of report, like financial statements, would be an information type report.

I know this is probably not exactly correct, but knowledge is information to which you've applied some kind of a theory or thinking.

Two examples I'll use here: any kind of a cash flow projection report. That's a knowledge report because what you're doing is you're basing it on a theory — if we get paid in the average days to pay and we're going to pay our people on time, then this is what the cash flow is going to look like. The theory, of course, is that we're going to get paid in an average number of days and we're going to pay our people.

The other one that a lot of people use in a CRM system is a sales projection or a pipeline report. It says, "Okay, here's the date, this is the size of the deal, $50,000; this is the date we think it's going to close, and this is the percentage chance that we think this has of actually closing." If you take all of those in aggregate, you can actually project, theoretically, what your revenue is going to be for a given period.

Those would be an example of knowledge reports. By the way, on the top of the pyramid, I put wisdom, and I don't think we'll ever get to wisdom reports.

Ron: I like that definition, and I like applying a theory to information to turn it into knowledge, since data, and to some extent even information, is only by definition about the past. This is something that George Gilder loves to say, "Knowledge is about the past, but entrepreneurialism is about the future," and that's where we get dynamism, innovation, and economic growth.

Just to bounce off what you said, the way I explain it, and it's much more simplistic than yours, "If all you had in front of you was a list of phone numbers with no context, no names, just phone numbers, that would be data. If you had the Yellow Pages, they gave it some context, names, addresses, businesses, all of that, then that's information; but then, if you start asking people for word of mouth recommendations about plumbers, then that's more knowledge. That's the simple way that I use to illustrate the differences.

Ed: Right. So talk about the fact that knowledge is not free.

Ron: Again, another great line from Thomas Sowell's book, _Knowledge and Decisions_, "The most severe constraint facing human beings in all societies and throughout history is inadequate knowledge for making the decisions that each individual in every organization has to make." That's fascinating because it really is a constraint, I mean knowledge is actually very expensive.

Ed: I want to point out here that Sowell's talking about knowledge; he's not talking about data. He's not talking about data, which is why I wanted to make that distinction earlier because I see a lot of people in the customers that we work with, they have this fixation on data. If we just have more and more data then that's somehow a substitute for knowledge, and if you go with the idea that knowledge is really information to which you're applying a theory, well no amount of data is ever going to solve that. You still have to apply thinking in terms of positing a theory and your belief about a future to any decision that you're going to make in any context.

Ron: Not to get off the topic here, but this is one of my problems with the whole big data craze is it's great to analyze all these trillions of bits of data, but it's a reflection of the past. It doesn't necessarily tell us our future. We can't collect data on something that's new.

Ed: Now, let's be cautious here because a lot of people say, "Oh, you're against big data?" No.

Ron: No, not at all.

Ed: What we're against is the over-obsession with looking at the data and not making some predictive assumptions about the future.

That's what people get hung up on. What we're seeing and saying is that people sometimes get stuck in this obsession with data. It's almost, in some cases, like a substance abuse problem.

The Physical Fallacy

Ron: Not only is knowledge not free, but another common misconception in economics is the physical fallacy: The idea that wealth resides in only tangible things, such as manufactured goods, gold, or natural resources. Thomas Sowell does a brilliant job in his works debunking this fallacy as well.

Ed: One of my favorite stories about that is Merv Griffin and the theme song to Jeopardy. Griffin was the producer of the show and this was when Jeopardy first came on back in the '60s. Somebody said, "We need some music for the time when people are writing down their answers during Final Jeopardy." So Merv, being the savant that he was, sits down at the piano and he knocks out nah-nah-nah-nah-nah-nah-nah. His estate is still getting checks, and last I checked it was between $70 and $80 million in royalties just from the theme song.

Ron: Isn't that amazing? It tells you the power of an idea and this is one of the most possibly counter-intuitive points that economists have been making for centuries, is that real wealth does not reside in physical things. It resides in imagination, creativity, innovation, and ideas, rather than things that are just physical representations of those ideas. It kind of runs against our intuition, doesn't it?

Ed: It sure does, but we see it over and over again in business. Just recently, WhatsApp was bought for approximately $19 billion. WhatsApp was forty guys and fifteen contract programmers in Georgia, the country not the state.

Ron: When you can create a company with less than 50 employees, or whatever it was in total that they had, and be bought for $19 billion, which might be more than the market cap of Boeing, or some other massive company, that tells you the world has definitely changed from an atom economy to the economy in mind.

One of my favorite examples is the movie *Gone with the*

Wind. Here's a movie on tape; it was released in 1939. Would you rather own the rights to that movie, or the most expensive car from 1939? By the way, the most expensive car from 1939 is an Auto Union Type D Audi Grand Prix. It sold for roughly 12 million Euros.

I'd rather have <u>the rights to *Gone with the Wind*</u>, but that's just an idea, that's just a service. It's not something physical and yet it contains much more wealth. The idea that only manufacturing creates real lasting wealth is nonsense on stilts.

Ed: There's just example after example of this. The way we want to bring this to the every day thought process in businesses is we have to make sure that we carve out some time for ideas, for thinking. First of all, growing our knowledge, our intellectual capital, which we'll talk more about later, but allowing people to think about things, to create some of these ideas and give it a shot.

Ron: That's what Einstein meant when he said, "Imagination is even more important than knowledge." Isn't that where all innovation comes from, imagination or tinkering around, or just dreaming? And that's how we get all these great new products and services.

Ed: The key is that these ideas, when they're shared, even if a particular idea is bad, it doesn't mean that when somebody talks about it or speaks about it, that it can't be improved upon by somebody else who says, "Well that might not work, but if we tweak it a little bit here, it could potentially turn into this whole other thing."

We need to make sure that we're doing that and that's buried a lot in businesses today; just sit there, do your job, don't talk, don't give us any thoughts; be efficient; we've got to keep those young Millennials in check because they keep coming up with these ideas and thinking around us.

Ron: The old joke in the Henry Ford factory, was, "Hey you guys, stop talking and get back to work," but in the knowledge economy, it may be the exact opposite, "Hey guys, get to work, start talking."

Ed: Absolutely.

Ron: Because when you start talking with each other, it's like ideas having sex.

Ed: I love that phrase. It's a <u>Matt Ridley</u> line, right?

Rival and Non-Rival Assets

Ron: Yes, from his book, <u>*The Rational Optimist*</u>. You bring up another really interesting point, Ed, that if you think about knowledge, the way I first heard this described, it's a <u>*non-rival* asset as opposed to a *rival* asset</u>. If I give you the tie off my shirt, well that's a rival asset; now you have it and I don't; but if I give you an idea or knowledge, now we both have it. I don't lose it when I give it to you and now you can take it, improve upon it, tweak it, make it even more valuable for your organization or your customers. It might even come back to me in some type of modified and improved form. In other words, there's no law of diminishing returns with knowledge. The more you give it away, the more it increases.

Ed: Even <u>Thomas Jefferson</u> recognized this. He talked about the idea of a candle, if you take my entire candle from me, then I don't have light; but if I just light your candle with mine, now we both have light and it doesn't diminish mine either.

This is so hard for people to get their mind around because the law of diminishing returns is so entrenched in business thinking today and we get stuck on that thinking that we have to protect these ideas.

Ron: I wonder if that goes back to caveman times where if you got to the berries first, there was less for me? But that's not the way it works with knowledge.

Ed: No. It's almost the exact opposite, but it's not obvious. We've talked about economists, but even they didn't see this coming, this economy in mind. They didn't see the knowledge economy coming. Adam Smith and all the rest, they believed in this diminishing returns idea because quite honestly, that's the way it had been for millennia.

Ron: If everything that surrounds you is represented in atoms it's hard not to think that the world is zero sum, but it's turned out not at all like that and it's definitely an economy in mind.

Self Sufficiency = Poverty

Ed: Absolutely. We have example after example of this, but let's talk a little bit about a book that you recently read. Talk about the class project.

Ron: There's an economics professor at George Mason University, and to illustrate how knowledge is dispersed throughout the economy, where no one of us is smarter than all of us, and how a free market handles knowledge, he assigns a class project to his undergraduate economics students, "I want you to make something from scratch that you normally buy."

Now you can imagine a bunch of college students, they're going to do things like make a radio, maybe an MP3 player, a lot of them brew beer. What they figure out, Ed, is that not only is this a pain in the you-know-what, it takes a lot of time and a lot of shoe leather driving to get all these things, but it costs a fortune and the quality is awful.

Ed: Alright, so a toaster from scratch that's what this guy ended up doing?

Ron: Yes. This guy wrote a book; his name is <u>Thomas Thwaites</u>, he was a design student in London and he wrote this book called <u>*The Toaster Project*</u>. I just got done reading this and it's just a great book.

The first thing he says is, "Well I wanted to make something from scratch, so I just picked a typical run-of-the-mill-household appliance, a toaster." So he goes down to an appliance store and his logic is, "If I picked the cheapest toaster, that will have the fewest parts and it will be the easiest to replicate."

He buys a toaster for approximately four pounds, it's like eight bucks, roughly, and he takes it apart. There's something like 157 parts in this toaster, you can even start to break down those and now all of a sudden you're at over 400 parts. There was 38 different materials, 17 were metal, 18 plastic, I mean he goes on and on and on with all the different types of components in this thing.

The other thing he said was, "It's not really true that we can make anything from scratch," and this is the line that really stuck with me; he quoted <u>Carl Sagan</u> who said, "Well, if you want to make an apple pie from scratch, the first thing you have to do is invent the universe."

It's probably not realistic to think that you can make a toaster from scratch. He ran into all these problems, such as, can I use electricity? Otherwise, you'd have to make your own electricity. Given those parameters, he went out, he spent nine months, he traveled 1,900 miles to different mines up in Scotland and Ireland to get metal. He even contacted British Petroleum to get some petroleum to make the plastic for the outer cover. He goes into detail on how he did all this and he's got pictures in the book.

It's a great book. I really enjoyed it. At the end of the day, it cost him $1,837 and it took him nine months and it didn't work. And we're talking a toaster that you and I can walk into <u>Target and buy for eight bucks</u>.

Ed: Wow!

Ron: It's just an incredible story and it just shows you how interdependent we are even for something as simple as a toaster. There's a great essay and this book was in the spirit of that essay. The essay is by a guy named <u>Leonard Read</u> called <u>*I, Pencil*</u>, written in the voice of a pencil.

It basically starts off by saying, "As a pencil, nobody in the world knows how to make me." Now that sounds like an astonishing statement, but it's not. Millions and millions of people are needed to make a pencil and everything that goes into it.

Ed: This goes back to Matt Ridley who points this out in his book, *The Rational Optimist*, this idea that <u>a hand axe and a computer mouse effectively look the same</u>. Show a picture of them from a distance, you couldn't necessarily tell one versus the other, especially if it's a wireless mouse. They're designed to fit the human hand. The big difference, of course, is that the hand axe could be something that can be crafted by one person, and maybe that person was a specialist. The knowledge for that was then passed on from person to person to person, but it's a one-to-one relationship.

It wasn't until we realized that if we begin to share this idea and this knowledge, it increased where we're able to create the computer mouse, which is similar to your toaster or *I, Pencil*. There's no way that an individual could possibly make it.

Ron: Right.

Ed: I just wanted to mention because Ron is very much a shy person and won't say this, but a lot of the material that we're talking about here is in one of his fantastic books called <u>*Mind Over Matter: Why Intellectual Capital is the Chief*</u>

Source of Wealth, which when I first read it, it just blew my mind. I personally think, Ron, that's your best book.

Ron: Thank you, Ed, it was definitely the hardest book to write because, as you know, this is a very, very complex topic to get your head around because it is so counter-intuitive.

Explicit and Tacit Knowledge

Ed: Absolutely. Tell us a little bit about explicit and tacit knowledge, Ron, because that's a big input into this.

Ron: Yes, the difference between _tacit knowledge and explicit knowledge_ is critical to understand. Explicit knowledge is something that you can get out of a book, you can get it from a PowerPoint presentation, a spreadsheet, a podcast, that would be explicit.

Ed: A radio show?

Ron: Definitely, that's explicit knowledge. Tacit knowledge is sticky. It's that stuff that's in your head. It's all the little tricks of the trade. It's the craftsman's way of knowing when to break the rules, or the surgeon who knows when to deviate from standard procedure. It's that tacit knowledge that's so expensive to transfer, which is one of Thomas Sowell's points.

Let's say you're an expert in something, I mean a deep, deep expert and you go on to Wikipedia. Now Wikipedia is a great example of an incredible database of explicit knowledge, but if you've got a lot of tacit knowledge about a particular topic, you'll see a lot of gaping holes in Wikipedia, won't you?

Ed: Oh, yeah. I have great example of this that I use around my house all the time. My wife, Christine, and I we're staying with friends up in Kansas City, this was five or six years ago I suppose, it might have been even longer than that; at one point, we get up and we needed to make another pot of coffee, right?

Our friends go to refill the coffee pot. They had positioned their coffee pot in such a way that it was within striking distance of the hose from the sink, so that you can just pull the hose from the sink to fill the coffee pot. This just struck me as absolute genius. How many times do you go fill the coffee pot, bring it over, then dump it in, right? It's just maddening. No, no, you move your coffee pot to within striking distance of the hose.

Well I've got to tell you that I think of them, first of all, every time I do it, which is just about every day and then also, the other thing that's cool is I have done this in front of other people who have said, "I'm going home and moving my coffee pot."

Ron: That's a great thing about a good idea.

Ed: But no expert on making coffee is going to tell you that. It's not going to show up in the research anywhere, it's not going to be in the data.

Ron: Right. If I read a book by Tiger Woods or Jack Nicklaus on how to play golf their way, that's explicit knowledge, but if you gave me the opportunity to go play a round with either of them, that's tacit knowledge because I'm going to get into all sorts of situations that aren't explained in their book, which is the stuff that's really, really valuable. That's really what Thomas Sowell was arguing when he said that knowledge is actually the biggest constraint. It's not ubiquitous, and it's not free.

Ed: In putting this into practice in organizations, one of the keys is to have, and you've told me this Ron, this idea of having a chief knowledge officer. You might not call them a CKO, but we need to have somebody who knows what everyone knows. This is why former Hewlett-Packard (HP) CEO Lew Platt said: "If HP knew what HP knows, we would be three times as profitable."

This is not someone who is on mission to know everything. They just know what other people know, and that that's something that every business needs to start to put into practice: who knows what we know around here.

Types of Intellectual Capital

Ron: Right, because intellectual capital, unlike physical capital or physical assets, because they're non-rival, they can be in more than one place at one time. We can all read Harry Potter's book at the same time without diminishing it for anybody else, then it starts to make sense to think about different types of intellectual capital. The best breakdown I've seen is by <u>Karl Sveiby</u>, he's Australian I believe, and in 1989, he broke out intellectual capital to three components.

He said, "Every business has *human capital*, this is what gets in the elevator every night and goes home. Every company has *structural capital* and you can think of that as everything that stays in the four walls after the people leave — databases, tools, methods, strategies, processes, etc. Then you've got *social capital*, which is the company's customers — a company's brand is part of its social capital since it's really owned by the customers — and alumni, vendors, organizations they are members of, and things like that.

I found that framework really useful to think about in terms of how do you leverage intellectual capital, because knowledge is an entity; it's not a process. Intellectual capital is knowledge that can be converted into profit. It's the interdependence of these three types of intellectual capital that can really create some serious wealth for your customers. And only one of the components, structural capital, is actually owned by the company.

Ed: In a sense, isn't social capital similar to what your grandmother probably told you, it's not what you know, it's who you know.

Ron: Absolutely. That is a big part of it and what's really fascinating, Ed, and this is something that the economists back in the day wouldn't have seen as dramatically as we see it now, is human capital, according to a <u>report by the World Bank</u> is 80% of the developed world's wealth — 80%!

If you think about it, that means that if you're in a knowledge business, and I would say almost every business has got some component of knowledge, but certainly professional firms, that means 80% of your ability to create wealth resides in your people, and the company does not own them.

Ed: No, not at all. Am I extrapolating this out too much, though? When I heard that 80% figure, I was completely blown away by it, but the way that I have internalized it is this, and I'm curious if you think my thinking is off. If that's true, if 80% of the world's wealth is in human capital, that means that if we actually did have a systemic financial crisis of absolutely epic proportion where we lost all financial wealth, which I don't think can possibly happen if we lose all financial wealth; but let's just say that it happened, that we would still as a species be able to continue as long as we continue to have our knowledge about the past. We could sustain that, we could sustain that colossal financial collapse, but what we couldn't sustain would be a disease that gives us amnesia.

Ron: You're absolutely right, if you think about it. If you were to decimate our physical infrastructure, I don't know, like the neutron bomb. Wasn't that the bomb that only destroyed people, not buildings?

Ed: Yeah. It only kills people.

Ron: But it keeps the buildings intact. Well if you reverse that. No, we would be able to rebuild as long as you don't lose that knowledge and that's what's so key about knowledge because you can't really lose it. You transfer it and it only grows.

By the way, the World Bank is the entity that did the studies on 80% of the world's wealth residing in human capital and there are two studies. The first one's called "Where is the Wealth of Nations," and the second is "The Changing Wealth of Nations."

Illustration by Andrew Fyfe

Ed: This just amazes me, though, this idea that 80% of wealth is in our human capital. At first, I doubted it, but the more and more I think about it, the more it makes complete and total sense. I mean after all, what is a brand, right? Knowledge that I can trust. I know that if I'm going to go into a McDonald's, I'm going to get a fast, barely edible meal, but I'm going to get it fast.

Ron: Yes, and something else that we should probably mention, too, is not all knowledge is good — not all of the components of intellectual capital are good. Some of them are negative; there's <u>negative human capital</u>, negative structural capital, and certainly negative social capital, like hanging out with the "wrong crowd."

The example I love about this is <u>Castro's</u> Cuba. Here's a guy who had expropriated all the wealth, the physical wealth, thinking, "Oh, I'm going to make the greatest city in the world," and he ended up doing that but he did it in Miami because all the human capital left. He created a great city in Miami and left Cuba to rot because he didn't understand that true wealth resided in the free minds of people. He believed in the physical fallacy, basically.

Ed: But don't businesses do this, too. Obviously, to a much lesser extent than Castro, when they castigate the people who used to work for them. Somebody leaves the organization and they just become like Yul Brenner as Ramses in *The Ten Commandments*, "Strike Moses's name from every obelisk." Anything that went wrong in the past 10 years, we blame on the guy who just left and I constantly see this happen. Unless the guy or gal was really a fool, why are we doing this to them? Why aren't we trying to maintain the relationship long-term, because you never know when this is going to be an example to use social capital that allows us to continue to connect.

Ron: Absolutely, Ed. For all the hard times that we like to give the large professional firms, one thing that they do absolutely right, and almost all of them do this, is they maintain an alumni network and they cultivate those relationships. They don't castigate you as you leave. They know you're probably going to go somewhere that can refer them future business and they understand the value of that social capital and they invest in it heavily.

Even my prior accounting firm, KPMG, has an incredible

alumni network that's quite active and actually provides a lot of value.

Ed: Yeah and I see that all of the time. It's funny you say that the professional firms get it, which is true in that particular case, but where it's not true is that they're among the last to adopt social media.

Ron: True.

Ed: Which to me is just the most modern form of social capital. I do social media not because it's cute, but because it's the best form of social capital that's ever been invented by mankind.

Ron: Ed, let's talk about knowledge workers because we hear this term a lot. Peter Drucker was the one who coined this term in 1959. He started to see a big influx into the labor force of people who basically work with their minds, not their muscles, and he coined the term knowledge workers.

What makes the knowledge worker unique as opposed to an industrial worker or a service worker, the defining trait is they *own the means of production*, and what a tectonic shift that is.

If I worked for Henry Ford back in the day, he owned the means of production; I went into his factory, I worked to the rhythms and cadences of his assembly line. Today, I don't have to go into an office. I can sit in a Starbucks and do a full day's work, as indeed JK Rowling wrote the first Harry Potter novel sitting in a coffee shop. That's the difference with knowledge workers, you own the means of production.

Ed: I have actually heard it said that way, that the way that you can tell if you're a full on knowledge worker is instead of bringing your coffee to the office, you can bring your office to the coffee.

Knowledge Workers are Volunteers

Ron: The other point that Drucker made about knowledge workers is the balance of economic power has shifted, organizations need them more than the knowledge workers need the organizations, because obviously these people have 80% of the capacity to create wealth that walks around with them. The best that companies can do is rent this human capital. Ultimately, these people are volunteers.

Ed: This is the distinguishing characteristic that I see between the service worker and the service economy and the knowledge economy, or the experience economy, whatever phrase we want to use; we've been calling it knowledge so we'll stick with that. This idea that it's the worker who owns the means of production. Let me use the airlines as an example, or a hotel, you still have to go to the airport; you still have to go to the McDonald's; you still have to go to the place of business.

With an accounting firm, with a law firm, with an IT firm, you don't have to go there anymore. That's knowledge, that value is with the person. Again, it's spiritual rather than physical.

Ron: It's much like when you invest your 401K, or whatever portfolio you have, you're going to invest your financial capital into those places where you'll get a fair economic return commensurate with risk, but also where your assets will be treated well. It's why you won't invest in Castro's Cuba because he might take your assets away, but it's the same thing for a knowledge worker. They're actually investing their own intellectual capital into a company and therefore, they're going to go where they're fairly compensated, of course, but also where they're treated with respect and dignity.

Of course, this is our problem with Taylorism. You didn't

treat the worker with respect and dignity, and Taylor has no place in the knowledge economy. (We will discuss this further in Chapter 3.)

Ed: Not at all. Just to continue this thought, this social capital, as you are aware, Ron, the Sage Company I work for, our conference is next week. This is always my most exciting week at work because I get a chance, first of all, to prepare for the talks that I'm going to do and gain greater knowledge; but then I get a chance to share it all with people and to have their knowledge be shared back with me. It's like this big explosion of knowledge that I quite literally have to spend the next month or two digesting.

Ron: It's an incredible enhancement to social capital, too. I haven't attended as many summits as you have, but I still have relationships with people that I met at summit years ago.

Ed: Yeah.

Ron: Let's talk a little bit about social capital, Ed, because one of the things that's interesting about human capital and social capital is neither of them are owned by the company. So a knowledge firm is actually a very asset-less organization. It really doesn't own the assets because you can't own human capital.

When you think about a brand, I always ask audiences who owns Coca-Cola's brand, and if you're talking to lawyers or accountants, they'll say, "Well the shareholders." That's true, legally, but from an economics standpoint, it's obviously the customers who own the brand because look what happened with new Coke.

Ed: Yeah, they almost destroyed it.

Ron: Another aspect of social capital that's very important is values that we transmit from one generation to another. Alvin Toffler used to stump and crack up audiences with the following question, "What's it worth to your organization that your people were potty-trained?"

Ed: A lot.

Ron: It's one of those great questions. A couple of other things to illustrate this very starkly is if you look at North and South Korea. You can obviously look at that satellite image at night where North Korea is completely blacked out while South Korea is lit up like a Christmas tree.

Ed: My iPad. My screensaver on my iPad reminds me of this.

Ron: Ed, there's an even better picture, one that came out of the Space Station that's even more dramatic. Here you have two countries that are the same language, the same culture, same history and look at the dramatic difference.

It's because one respects freedom, dignity, liberty, and unleashes their people to be their best and one is just a tyranny of materialism and a great example of the physical fallacy. They have all the natural resources up in North Korea. They have the mines and all these natural resources but they don't have the knowledge to get it out and do anything with it.

It's a great illustration of the physical fallacy versus the knowledge economy that we've been talking about.

Ed: It was only really unleashed in the South in about 1980. Before that, they were certainly freer, I suppose, but in some ways equally oppressive. It's only once they figured it out, "Oh, this is what we have to do in order to grow this," that they made the leap in growth.

It is a great example, Ron, of negative social, structural, and human capital. This is just evil. I just read a book called _Dear Reader_ and I almost spent too much time on it, we could do a whole show on it. This is the unauthorized autobiography of <u>Kim Jong Il</u>, which shows you how evil the thinking is and why they're not crazy. One of the other things that the author, <u>Michael Malice</u>, points out is that we have to stop thinking of these people as crazy; they're not crazy. There is a logic to it, they're just evil.

Ron: I read that book, too, and it was a fascinating book, you're right. If you really want a stark image of the knowledge economy, look at President <u>Ronald Reagan's best speech</u>, which he delivered in 1988, the last year of his presidency, at Moscow State University, Mikhail Gorbachev's alma mater (reproduced in the Introduction).

He's standing in front of a bust of Lenin and a mural of the Russian Revolution and he's basically telling the students, ever so kindly, that their country is destined for the ash heap of history. He doesn't say it that bluntly, he says it very nice but he's explaining what he calls the information economy that's actually the knowledge economy.

He actually quotes this book that was written in 1982 called *The Economy in Mind*, by Warren T. Brookes, who's no longer with us. He's probably one of the reasons, Ed, along with George Gilder and Thomas Sowell, that I wrote my book, *Mind over Matter*, and probably why we're doing this show, *The Soul of Enterprise: Business in the Knowledge Economy*.

Next, let's explore one of the most effective ways for capturing and disseminating intellectual capital throughout your organization, or what Ed and I refer to as the best learning tool ever invented — the after action review.

Supplemental Material

According to Alvin and Heidi Toffer, there are five eras we have moved through in society:

1. Hunters & gatherers economy

2. Agrarian economy

3. Industrial economy

4. Service economy

5. Knowledge economy (often referred to as the "Information economy," but this is a misnomer)

There's an enormous difference between information and knowledge. Again, Thomas Sowell explains why knowledge, far from being free, is enormously expensive, and the most severe constraint facing societies:

[T]he most severe constraints facing human beings in all

societies and throughout history — inadequate knowledge for making all the decisions that each individual and every organization nevertheless has to make, in order to perform the tasks that go with living and achieve the goals that go with being human.

Data, Information and Knowledge

Data. Factual information (as measurements or statistics) used as a basis for reasoning, discussion or calculation. There is no judgment, interpretation, context, or basis for action. It knows nothing of its own importance or irrelevance.

Information. Root in Latin is *formare*, meaning "to shape." Peter Drucker said information is "data endowed with relevance and purpose." It has to have a sender and a receiver, and it is the receiver, not the sender, who decides if the message is information or not. "We add value to information in various ways: Contextualized; Categorized; Calculated; Corrected; Condensed"

Knowledge. The fact or condition of knowing something with familiarity gained through experience or association. To turn information into knowledge we need: "Comparison; Consequences; Connections; Conversation.

Rival and Non-Rival Assets

Alvin and Heidi Toffler define characteristics of knowledge in their book *Revolutionary Wealth*:

1. Knowledge is inherently non-rival
2. Knowledge is intangible
3. Knowledge is non-linear
4. Knowledge is relational
5. Knowledge mates with other knowledge — ideas having sex
6. Knowledge is more portable than any other product
7. Knowledge can be compressed into symbols or abstractions
8. Knowledge can be stored in smaller and smaller spaces

9. Knowledge can be explicit or implicit, expressed or not expressed, shared or tacit
10. Knowledge is hard to bottle up. It spreads.

Knowledge is like the dark matter of the cosmos—we know it there, but we cannot see, touch, or measure it.

Again, Thomas Sowell:

Many of the products that create a modern standard of living are only the physical incorporation of ideas — not only the ideas of an Edison or Ford but the ideas of innumerable anonymous people who figure out the design of supermarkets, the location of gasoline stations, and the million mundane things on which our material well-being depends. It is those ideas that are crucial, not the physical act of carrying them out. Societies which have more people carrying out physical acts and fewer people supplying ideas do not have higher standards of living. Quite the contrary. Yet the physical fallacy continues on, undaunted by this or any other evidence.

Types of Intellectual Capital

Intellectual Capital is defined as *Knowledge that can be converted into profits (or value)*; it's an entity, not a process.

Intellectual Capital was classified into three categories by Karl-Erik Sveiby, in 1989:

1. Human capital (HC). This comprises your team members and associates who work either for you or with you. As one industry leader said, this is the capital that leaves in the elevator at night. The important thing to remember about HC is that it **cannot be owned**, only contracted, since it is completely volitional. In fact, more and more, knowledge workers **own the means of your company's production**, and knowledge workers will invest their HC in those organizations that pay a decent return on investment, both economic and psychological. In the final analysis, your **people are not assets** (they deserve more respect than a copier machine and a computer), they are not **resources** to be harvested from the land like coal when you run out; ultimately, they are *volunteers* and it is totally up to them whether or not they get back into the elevator the following morning.

2. Structural capital. This is everything that remains in your company once the HC has stepped into the elevator, such as databases, customer lists, systems, procedures, intranets, manuals, files, technology, and all of the explicit knowledge tools you utilize to produce results for your customers.

3. Social capital. This includes your customers, the main reason a business exists; but it also includes your suppliers, vendors, networks, referral sources, alumni, joint venture and alliance partners, reputation, and so on. Of the three types of IC, this is perhaps the **least leveraged**, and yet it is highly valued by customers.

There is such a thing as *negative* human capital, *negative* structural capital, and *negative* social capital. Not everything we know is beneficial.

Think of the IC a thief possesses and the social loss they impose is a societal negative.

Examples of negative intellectual capital in an organization: cost-plus pricing, Industrial Age efficiency metrics, Taylorism (see Chapter 3), focusing on activities and costs rather than results and value, and other forms of negative IC that have embedded themselves into the culture.

On Knowledge Workers

Knowledge workers are unique:

- They *own* the means of production
- Firms need them more than they need firms — the balance of power has shifted
- Knowledge workers have unique value, not jobs
- The office is their servant, not their master

- *Effectiveness* is far more important than *efficiency*
- *Judgments* are more important than **measurements**
- Ultimately, they are **volunteers**

Chapter 2: <u>The Best Learning Tool Ever Invented</u>

The Army's After Action Review is arguably one of the most successful organizational learning methods yet devised.

— Peter Senge

Ed: Ron, on our last show we talked about our "Top Ten Business Myths," what do you think went well?

Ron: The fact that we got all ten of them in was a great accomplishment.

Ed: It was two shows though.

Ron: It was, but it could have been many more. That went really well, I thought.

Ed: Okay. Anything else that you think went well?

Ron: I thought we discussed some really good content, and what I really enjoyed about the show is how all of these myths altered our thinking. We might have at one point in our professional careers believed in some of these myths, but our minds have been changed by empirical evidence, and that was a good lesson as well.

Ed: I liked the fact that we gave some really strong business examples for our audience specifically.

What do you think did not go so well, Ron?

Ron: Well, you always think, "I could have used a better example," or "I could explain this in a more clear way with a better metaphor, or a better analogy." This is one of the things that we do after every show, right? We talk about how we could have said that better. I guess it's like an actor reviewing the scene: "I flubbed that line," or "I could have moved this way or turned that way." You can always use better stories and explain yourself more clearly.

Ed: The last question that we should really talk about in doing this — what is really an informal after action review — is, "What's the one thing that we're going to do different next time to make an improvement?"

Ron: All this is about this process of the after action review (AAR). Why don't we get into this, Ed, and talk about where this comes from and why we even want to do it? Maybe even back up before the AAR; what are we trying to accomplish by having this conversation?

Ed: We're trying to live what we preach. Folks, Ron and I really do conduct an AAR almost immediately following every show. Why? Because we want to get better. We want to improve our condition, but we also want to improve the human condition and we think that what we have to say on *The Soul of Enterprise* is valuable, and we just want to make sure that we have a great product for you to consume on a regular basis. At least that is it for me, Ron, but is it something else for you?

Ron: No. I want this show to be a worthwhile investment because I know people's time is precious. They could spend it doing many different things, and if they're going to spend this hour with us, then I want to make that return on investment very, very high.

I suppose, Ed, one of the reasons why we do this and one of the reasons this show is subtitled *Business in the Knowledge Economy* is because we know how important knowledge is, and knowledge is what we're trying to capture with these AARs. I love what <u>Andrew Carnegie</u> said, "The only irreplaceable capital an organization possesses is the knowledge and ability of its people. The productivity of that capital depends on how effectively people share their competence with those who can use it." That's really what the AAR is designed to do, to share that knowledge and share that learning and competence.

Ed: Absolutely. Capturing that knowledge because it really is something that's fleeting, isn't it? There's for sure a half-life to it. One of the reasons why we like to do our AAR right after the show is because otherwise we'll forget, and if we do it even one day later, it's going to be half as good as if we did it immediately.

Ron: Right. It's like interviewing witnesses at a crime scene. You know you want to get to them right away, otherwise memories fade, things change, and you lose some of this learning.

Ed: Exactly. We both feel that the AAR is the best knowledge management and learning tool that has been designed by mankind. Period.

Ron: Yes. Ever.

Knowledge Lessons from the U.S. Army

Ed: Let's talk a little bit about the history of these AARs. They've got a very interesting history, mostly from the United States Military. Interesting corporation, that.

Ron: Yes. Usually, we don't look at military organizations because, let's face it, their mission is to kill people and break things, and we don't think of them as knowledge organizations; but in this case the United States Army was the first of our branches of the military to introduce the AAR in its current format.

I do believe that the military branches have always done these debriefing exercises, but the idea of formalizing it actually came into play in the United States Army, and it was done around the early 1970s.

Ed: It was really a response to Vietnam, wasn't it?

Ron: It was. It was because the morale in the military was so low and they thought they could increase it, along with the ethical framework, by requiring these AARs. It took them a few years to figure it out, but what they realized was, "This is an incredible knowledge tool that we can use that not only makes us more efficient, but more effective in our operations," and so they really became quite committed to it.

Ed, there's a great book on this. It's called *Hope is Not a Method*. It's by two guys, Gordon R. Sullivan and Michael V. Harper. It's the definitive historical look at AARs because it was Gordon Sullivan, he was former Army Chief of Staff, and he's the one that actually implemented AARs, and he talks about the struggle and how this is a big cultural change. It took him a long time to get this into the culture.

Ed: Decades. They've been doing them since the early '70s, but my understanding is it wasn't until late in the 1980s, and maybe really with the first Gulf War in 1991, where these really became so prevalent and ubiquitous, or I should say embraced by the actual commanders and people on the ground.

Lost and Obsolete Knowledge

Ron: Right. If we just step back for a minute, and I know it's kind of a bizarre example, but think of the Stradivarius violin. Even with all of our modern technology and our 3D printing and 3D imaging in computers and all of that, we cannot to this day replicate a Stradivarius violin. We've tried many times — this is known as the "Stradivarius secret."

Just imagine if Antonio Stradivari would have done AARs, some of this knowledge might have survived and we may be able to replicate his violin. That's really what we're trying to do. We're trying to capture this knowledge because if you think about the aging workforce, we have all these really, really smart people for the first time retiring in waves from organizations, and not only are we going to lose their day-to-day labor, we're going to lose their knowledge.

How do you capture that knowledge so the younger folks can have access to it and be able to do their jobs more effectively? That's really what the AAR is designed to do in a business context.

Ed: Right, capture that knowledge. There's a interesting term out there. Alvin and Heidi Toffler coined it: _Obsoledge_ — Obsolete knowledge.

What they mean by that is the stuff that really is not useful anymore. Herbert Hoover's hat size no longer really needs to be preserved through the annals of history.

Ron: Right, or we don't have to learn how to use a slide rule anymore.

Ed: Right, but there is this knowledge that exists with these folks that are out there now, and as you say, who are getting closer to retirement age every day — the baby boomers. That is important knowledge, and look at a specific example of, say, going to the moon. It's my understanding we don't know how to go anymore. We would have to reinvent our way to the moon.

Ron: That's right. NASA actually admits that they've lost this knowledge. Now, some of that's good because, obviously, the technology that we would use to get to the moon today is going to be much different than what we used in the past, but it is interesting when you think about that specific example that you can lose that type of knowledge. Where does it go?

Ed: There's two different types of knowledge: tacit and explicit. Could you maybe explain those two?

We Know More Than We Can Tell

Ron: This is best illustrated — I just love this story — by a teacher who tells one of his pupils to write a letter to his parents, and the student complains, "It's hard for me to write a letter." The teacher says, "Why is it so hard? You're a year older now." (We're talking like second or third grade). He says, "Yes, but a year ago, I could say everything I knew."

It's obvious that we all know more than we can tell. This was said by <u>Michael Polanyi</u>, who was at one point Albert Einstein's research assistant, and then turned into a philosopher. He drew a distinction between tacit and explicit knowledge. To illustrate this, think about explaining to somebody how to ride a bike or how to swim.

Yes, you can intellectualize it to a point, but it's very tacit knowledge to know how to ride a bike. Whereas explicit knowledge is something that you can get from reading a book, or from watching a video, or a PowerPoint presentation, or looking at a spreadsheet, and so forth. That's explicit knowledge where we can put it somewhere, we can reuse it later, but tacit knowledge is that sticky stuff that's in your head that's really hard to draw out. I do think this is a fascinating distinction.

Ed: It's beyond just the physical, too, because as you were going through that, I'm thinking with my son, "Okay. I can explain to him Babe Ruth had 713 home runs, Hank Aaron had 755, Barry Bonds, etcetera," and that's explicit knowledge, right?

Ron: Right.

Ed: Last night, we're at practice and we're just moving from coach pitch to kid pitch. The difficulty all of them are having with the concept is that, "Okay, the ball is not going to always be over the plate like it was in coach pitch" (although, in all fairness, I did hit a couple of kids, including my own). For the most part, when the coach was pitching to him, they knew that it was going to be pretty much near the strike zone. Now, they have to incorporate a couple of different factors.

First of all, "Is the ball in the strike zone or not?" Right? Here's the hard part. If you're going to hit a baseball, and this is what we were working on last night, you have to assume that it is in the strike zone, right? What we keep telling them is "Assume a swing." We tell them, "Think yes."

The whole idea behind the swing is "Yes. Yes. Yes. Yes. Yes. Yes", and then at the last second, "No" because you see that it's a ball, because if you wait until you decide if it's a ball or a strike to decide, "Yes, I've got to swing," you're too late.

Ron: The opportunity is gone.

Ed: I can't tell you how often this happens in business. Right? Consider analyzing the data, the endless backward looking at data to be able to make a decision is a lot like, "Is it a strike or is it not?" You've got to be thinking, "Yes," right?

You'd be thinking "Yes," and then maybe you back out at the last second and say, "No," but there's a lesson in there.

Ron: There's a great lesson in there. In fact, they talk about explicit knowledge being low bandwidth, like reading a book by Jack Nicklaus on how to golf. Actually playing golf with Jack Nicklaus would be tacit knowledge, which is very high bandwidth, but it also illustrates the point that tacit knowledge is *dynamic*, whereas explicit knowledge is *static*. If we publish a book, that knowledge is very static, and at some point, it might become obsolete. Hence, Alvin Toffler's great, awkward word...

Ed: Obsoledge.

Ron: Yes, obsoledge, which is very true. There's a lot of knowledge that's completely obsolete and wouldn't do us any good. That's really what Polanyi was saying, that we need to draw this distinction because what's fascinating about this, Ed, in the Internet age, people say, "Information wants to be free," and that's true. To some extent, you can even get explicit knowledge off of the Internet. I can go to the Mayo Clinic or WebMD.com and, even as a layperson, I can learn certain things about various ailments or diseases, but I don't have that tacit knowledge that my doctor has.

Ed: What my doctor refers to as "Doctor Google." I walk into his office and I'm like, "I've got a tumor." He's like, "Ed, you've been going to 'Dr. Google' again, haven't you?" I'm like, "Yes. It started off with a light fever, and then..." "Okay. That's everything from the common cold to Ebola, all right?"

Ron: Right.

Ed: Stop going to Dr. Google.

Ron: I love the French saying, *"je ne sais quoi,"* which means, "I don't know what." In other words, it's very hard to articulate tacit knowledge. It's like you can't describe <u>Marilyn Monroe's face</u>, but if I showed you hundreds of pictures, you'd be able to pick her out almost instantaneously.

Ed: It's interesting how we humans do that as opposed to a computer, because we would scan. We wouldn't have to look at every single picture, whereas a computer algorithm would have to go through every photo until it found Marilyn. Admittedly, it can do it really fast.

This is the whole idea of why it is that a <u>chess program can now beat the best chess player</u> because we have gotten to the point where the machines are so quick. They're still not as creative, however. They still don't have the ability to create something new.

Ron: The other interesting thing about tacit knowledge is it's a social process between individuals. It'd be very difficult to do an AAR by yourself. You could do it, and you could turn some of that tacit knowledge into explicit knowledge, but when there's more than one mind working together, that's when you start sharing that sticky, hard-to-describe knowledge.

Ed: Right. I absolutely believe that you have to conduct an AAR with another person. I suppose, in theory, you could sit down and answer the questions. I always encourage people when I'm teaching this topic to do this with someone, even if they're a sole proprietor. They should go through the AAR process with a spouse, significant other, a brother, a sister, a mother, it doesn't matter. Have someone just talk this through with you. They say, "What if they didn't participate in the project?" I say, "That's great. It doesn't matter."

Ron: It might even better, because then they're not attached to anything. The other thing, in "The Economy in Mind" (Chapter 1), we discussed three types of intellectual capital: *human capital*, and that's 80% of the developed world's wealth these days, so this is why we call the show what we do, but why we focus so much on knowledge workers and intellectual capital. Second, there's *social capital*, which is obviously customers, vendors, your relationships, networks and all of that, but there's also *structural capital*. That's the stuff that stays inside of your firm after the humans go home at night.

What's interesting about the AAR is it's designed to get that human capital out of our heads and put it somewhere so we can put it into the structural capital and reuse it. That's really what the AAR is designed to do in a business setting.

Ed: Something as crazy as the cave paintings in, where is it, Lascaux, France? I'm firmly convinced that those were either a SWOT analysis, or perhaps an AAR. "Here's how the hunt went. The antelope had the horns, but we (humans) had the bows and arrows, and this is why this was better for us." In a sense we can get knowledge from eons ago when it's properly converted from social capital into structural capital.

Ron: And now, with the digital age, this is so much easier because we can just put an iPhone on the table and either video or record an AAR. We no longer have to have a reporter there. AARs used to be typed up in the Army's old days. Now, there's so many ways to capture this and store them on blogs, intranets, and all sorts of different types of media platforms, which are all searchable, so these become much more effective tools to use.

Ed: Right, and even converting them over to text from that point — just record them as an MP3 and use a service to convert it to text file because one of the advantages to text is that it can be read at four or five times the speed than someone who's listening to it.

Never Build the Same Bridge Twice

Ron: When I first ran across the AAR, it was over a decade now, to me, it was just like one of those 'Ah-ha' moments. I thought back to all of the experiences in my career when I redid something and I reinvented the wheel that had already been done a million times simply because I didn't know where the knowledge was, or who to ask.

I ended up going down a much steeper learning curve because of that, and I thought, "Oh, geez. If we would have had this, it would have made us a heck of a lot more effective."

What I'd like to do is just quickly explain the Army's philosophy, and I got this out of the *Hope is Not a Method* book, which folks, if you're interested in using the AAR and implementing it in your organization, please get hold of this book. It really is a fantastic book. Plus, it's got a lot of very interesting historical military examples, which I absolutely loved.

It's in that book where they say, "The Army never wants to build the same bridge twice." What this means is, say you had a platoon that was given the task of building a bridge to move troops, tanks, and the like. Yes, they can take out the Army manuals, go to the site, start to build the bridge, and the Army manual will tell them how to build the specific bridge, but one of the things it's not going to be able to tell them is all the little tricks of the trade, such as the Army manual says to use this joint or this type of weld, but in reality, this works better, so all those little things that you learn, all that tacit, sticky knowledge.

What happens now is after that platoon builds that bridge, they come back and they do an AAR. So then when another platoon on the other side of the planet is given the exact same task to go build that type of bridge, now the first thing they do is search the Army's databases for AARs on building that type of bridge. They read those first, or maybe they listen to them, but that's going to make that second bridge built much more efficiently, but more importantly, more effectively. That's really what they're trying to do. Imagine if you could do that in organizations.

Ed: That's exactly what we've designed our AAR Agenda to do (see Supplemental Material at the end of this chapter). In an organization, whether it's primarily a knowledge organization or not, you've got knowledge workers in it, so if you're in the service economy or the manufacturing economy, you're going to have areas in your company where the AAR is going to be the best tool to use. Just to take you through the process, we strongly encourage a couple of things. One, that you have a separate facilitator and a separate scribe, because the facilitator really needs to make sure that the process is followed. This is one of the things that I mentioned earlier, which is that sometimes it's best for this person to not have been associated with whatever the engagement matter was, that they be somebody different just because they have got to keep the discussion on track. We also think that having a scribe separate from that role is important.

Just a quick word on scribes. This does not mean that they are taking dictation like a court recorder on *Law & Order*, writing every word that is said. The scribe is really there to capture the insights. We also believe that this should be recorded so that you can have folks go back and listen to them after the fact.

Imagine if your organization could go back and listen to AARs that were created five years ago when this technology already existed. The other important point to mention before you begin the AAR is to tell people that they should have thought about the answers to the questions that we're going to talk to about *before* they get to the meeting. You don't want folks to get to the meeting and have them saying, "Okay, what went well? Let me think about that."

There are a couple of other ground rules that really come from the military. The first is they say to go through the ground rules. One of the ground rules is to go through the ground rules, and that's because that in the military, what they're worried about is insubordination, things like that.

The big number one ground rule is that AARs are for learning, not criticism, and that you're absolutely not allowed to attack anyone personally, and that no hierarchy exists during the meeting. In other words, there's no such thing as insubordination in questioning the actions of the superior during an AAR. There still is during the actual action, but during the AAR, you are allowed to, in fact strongly encourage to do so. One of the things that the field manual says is, "Make sure that you have the junior folks speak first." That's an important lesson — you should really have the people in your organization who maybe had less interaction with this particular project speak first.

They should talk first because if you allow the people who had the most interaction to dominate the conversation, just like in the Army, if the Major says this, the Sergeant is going to say, "Yes, pretty much what the Major said."

Ron: Ed, they actually remove their caps because there's no rank in an AAR, either.

Ed: They do. I was told this fascinating story by someone who has done two tours of duty in Iraq. When they do an AAR, they take off their hats and put them rank down on the table to signify that, temporarily, they have relinquished their rank, which if any of you have done time in any branch of the service know that that's a big deal.

Ron: By the way, I just love how on your agenda that you want folks to bring at least three things that they think went well and three things that they think could have gone better. Just in my defense, Ed, you sprung the AAR on me at the start of the show, so I didn't have time to think about these things.

Ed: I know. I broke my own rule, right?

Ron: Yes. If you think about it ahead of time, it helps a lot more.

Ed: Sometimes I feel that going through those ground rules, even though they're probably more pertinent to the military, makes sense in a business context as well just to remind people. Then, the first real question that's asked is, "What were the objectives of whatever this was?" (Again, this project, engagement, matter, or whatever it is that you call it inside your organization). What's interesting about this question is that a lot of folks come back and say, "You know what? It was unclear what the objectives were."

Here's a big no-no in the Army. That's not going to fly. That is perhaps one of the first learnings that any organization that implements AARs learns is that they quickly need clarity of objective around anything and everything that they do, and if they just get that out of the AAR, it's a win-win across the board.

Ron: You mentioned how organizations can do this no matter what type of work, service or manufacturing. I've read some things on how Toyota conducts AARs. They spend a lot of time thinking about and communicating the objectives. If Toyota actually produces a car that exceeded what its objectives were, they actually don't sit around and pop champagne bottles and celebrate. They worry about why their objectives weren't right in the first place. It's pretty intense actually.

Ed: Ron, take us through the next set of questions?

Ron: After "What were the objectives?," because we make plans and then obviously somebody laughs and reality kicks in, the next is "What actually happened?" What the Army refers to as the "ground truth." Why was it different? What actually happened out there, and why was it different than our plans were?

Then, we analyze that in a little bit more detail by saying, "What went well?" And then, "Why did these things go well? What could have gone better?" and "Why did these things go wrong?" It's like you're looking at the positive things that diverted from the objectives and also the negative things. Then, "What are we going to do different next time?"

Then, Ed, I've seen this in other sources as well, the last question that they use is, "How are we going to do it better next time?"

Ed: Correct.

Ron: Very simple questions. The Army even has recommended time limits that you should spend on each of these questions, don't they?

Ed: They do. No AAR is really meant to last more than an hour because that's when people start to lose interest and it starts to become less valuable. It's really a distillation of the knowledge that we're trying to extract from this engagement. A couple of things that I wanted to point out about the questions is the great contribution the Army made was the addition of the "why" questions.

I have sat through plenty of what we used to call "Post-implementation meetings," where we pat ourselves on the back and talk about what went well and what could have gone better, but then there was no action taken on that learning. The Army, by inserting those "Why" questions, is really the great contribution, as well as the, "What we're going to do different next time?"

I have a little twist on the AAR when I'm working with organizations on implementation. The Army will let you do two, three, four, or five things differently. One of the things that I like to do with the, "What are we going to do different next time?" is implement what's called the "Curly Rule." Do you remember the movie *City Slickers*?

They asked Curly, "<u>Curly, what's the secret of life</u>?" He replies, "One thing."

The power behind the AAR in a knowledge worker environment, especially when you're first implementing them, is the "Curly Rule" — one thing, not 17 things.

What's the one thing you're going to do different next time, and how are you going to implement that? If you just fix that one thing over and over and over and create a culture of AARs in your organization, then you're going to be much better off.

Ron: On recommended times, the Army suggests no more than an hour. They do have a rule: 25, 25, 50, which is 25% reviewing what happened, 25% reviewing why it happened, and then the remaining 50% on what to do about it and how can you learn from it to improve for next time.

Another interesting point I learned from the book, *Hope is Not a Method*, is the objective of these AARs is not just to correct *things*, but rather to correct *thinking*, because the Army has learned that *flawed assumptions are the largest factor in flawed execution.*

That's just another way of saying one of our favorite mantras: *"There is no good way to execute a bad idea."*

Illustration by <u>Andrew Fyfe</u>

They're really going after thinking here in some of the assumptions behind the objectives, rather than just talking about how to build the bridge better. That's certainly a part of it, and that's going to happen as a natural consequence of asking some of these questions, but then the why questions dig behind that and get to the thinking behind it. It's like <u>Toyoda's five Whys</u>, right? If you keep asking why?, like a little kid does, that really gets to the heart of the issue.

Ed: It does.

Ron: Ed, I know you've facilitated a lot of these AARs because you really love to do it, and I have too, and it is fun, especially if you weren't involved in the project and you're just acting as the facilitator. You really do see the transformation in people's thinking, but I understand you do this in your family.

AAR with the Kids

Ed: Yes. This is really sort of twisted, but it's been a fascinating journey. I teach this class on a fairly regular basis about consulting theory in practice, and one of the last things I talk about is the AAR. The class ends on a Thursday, and when I deliver the class in Dallas, I'm able to get home in time for dinner.

This happened about five years ago. My son, who's now nine, was three, going to be four. We're sitting around dinner, and I'm still pondering this whole AAR concept. As we sit down, I turned to my son and I say, "Sean, what went well today?" My wife, Christine is like, "Oh God."

Ron: Rolled her eyes...

Ed: Yes. Like, "Really?"

We kept it simple. We did not go through the whys, but I did ask him, "So, what went well today?" He came up with something. Then I said, "So, what was bad today?" I'll always remember what he said, "It was a windy day, and when I got out of the car, the car door came and it slammed my hand." Now, fortunately, he did not get his hand caught in the door. It just grazed his hand on the way by.

He said it hurt a lot. I'm like, "All right, buddy. What are you going to do different tomorrow?" He processed this for a little bit, and he said, "I guess before I get in the car, I could go outside and go to the end of the driveway and see how windy it is, and if it's real windy, I'm going to make sure to move real fast away from the car when I get out of it." I'm like, "Okay. Life skill #17 accomplished. I'm a successful parent!"

Ron: At three, yes. That's pretty good.

Ed: The kid is now thinking, "How can I not injure myself?" That's good. That's a good skill. The next night came, and I was having fun with this, so I asked him the same thing. I forgot what the answers were. That was Friday night. Saturday night rolls around, and by this point, it had lost its luster a little bit, but halfway through dinner, Sean turns to me and says, "So, dad. What went well?"

He liked this game. He thought this was fun and turned the tables on me pretty quickly. What's cool about this is this is now the <u>standard dinner conversation at the Kless household</u>. We did it last night because we had the opportunity to have dinner together, and I do a lot of travel so it doesn't always happen with me, but I assure you that it now happens on a regular basis even when I'm not there, and we've introduced Cara to the family who's now five. I can tell you with absolute certainty that this has, without question, made for a better familial experience, and both my spouse, Christine, and I think that we're better parents because of it and that our kids tend, not always, but tend to be more mature than their counterparts, and do look at things in a little bit different light because of this process.

Ron: That's awesome. In a business context, we're all so busy and we move quickly from one thing to another, and we just don't take the time to step back and *reflect*, which comes from the Latin verb, meaning *refold*. Because reflection without action would be *passivity*, but action without reflection is *thoughtlessness*. If you combine action with reflection, then you're going to end up with learning that lasts, and that's the big advantage from the AAR. As usual, Yogi Berra said it best in the context of Bill Dickey, "Yes, Bill Dickey. He's learning me all his experience."

Ed: Yes.

Ron: Which is exactly what the AAR is designed to do. This is a cultural change, because this isn't just about technology. This is something that you actually have to embed in the culture, as the Army experienced, and it really is about learning and doing things better. One of the consequences I've seen from these is it drives out fear, because if you're really willing to sit around and talk about these questions, then it's going to drive out fear. You're no longer afraid to make mistakes or to screw up.

I love what surgeons say. They have a great philosophy when you make a mistake as a surgeon, "Forgive and remember," and the AAR enables you to do both of those.

Supplemental Material

To obtain a Microsoft Word version of Ed's After Action Review Agenda, visit https://drive.google.com/file/d/0BzO2ncfld4O2WDlOcURuS19Td3c/view?usp=sharing

Part 2 – The 'Effing' Debate: Efficiency vs. Effectiveness

Chapter 3: <u>Declaring Independence from the Tyranny of Taylorism</u>

Efficiency means focus on costs. But the optimizing approach should focus on effectiveness.

Effectiveness focuses on opportunities to produce revenue, to create markets, and to change the economic characteristics of existing products and markets. ...It then asks, To what results should, therefore, the resources and efforts of the business be allocated so as to produce extraordinary results rather than the "ordinary" ones, which is all efficiency can possibly produce?

This does not deprecate efficiency. Even the healthiest business, the business with the greatest effectiveness, can well die of poor efficiency. But even the most efficient business cannot survive, let alone succeed, if it's efficient in doing the wrong things, that is, if it lacks effectiveness. No amount of efficiency would have enabled the manufacturer of buggy whips to survive.

Effectiveness is the foundation of success — efficiency is a minimum condition for survival after success has been achieved.

Efficiency concerns itself with the input of effort into all areas of activity. Effectiveness, however, starts out with the realization that in business, as in any other social organism, 10 or 15 percent of the phenomena — such as products, orders, customers, markets, or people — produce 80 to 90 percent of the results.

The other 85 to 90 percent of the phenomena, no matter how efficiently taken care of, produce nothing but costs (which are always proportionate to transactions, that is, to busy-ness).

— Peter Drucker, <u>*People and Performance*</u>

Ed: *We hold these truths to be self-evident that all value is subjective, that the customer is the soul arbiter of value, which we in Enterprise create, and it is price that determines costs, not the opposite, that to secure these truths, policies and procedures are instituted among knowledge workers, and that whatever whenever any policy becomes destructive of these principles, it is the right of the knowledge worker to alter and abolish it, and to institute new policies laying its foundation on such principles as shall seem most likely to affect their creativity, dignity, self-respect, and happiness.*

Happy Independence Day, Ron!

Ron: Yes. You too, Ed.

(Editors note: The Independence Day references in this Chapter are from our first show, which aired July 4, 2014.)

What is Taylorism?

Ed: We're declaring our independence from the tyranny of Taylorism. Who is this guy, Frederick Winslow Taylor and why are we declaring our independence from this dude?

Ron: This is an amazing story. The ghost of Taylorism still casts a very long shadow. This guy was born in 1856, and he basically was the guy who ran around and did the time and motion studies in steel mills and factories, and he's credited with increasing the efficiency of the industrial era. He's credited with a lot of things, but he was sort of the world's first business consultant. He charged $35 a day, and he's a classic example of the type of thinker that just as Oliver Wendell Holmes wrote, "A hundred years after he's dead and forgotten men who never heard of him will be moving to the measure of his thought." That is certainly true to this day.

To this day in business enterprises around the world, we pay tribute to the ghost of Taylorism, or what I call the "Gospel of Efficiency" because everybody declares that we need to be more efficient.

Ed: It's really a "Cult of Efficiency," Ron. That's my observation. Wasn't it Holmes who actually coined the term "Scientific Management" on which Taylor's book was written?

Ron: Yes, he did. In fact, he was a big promoter of Taylorism and thought it would make government more efficient, make business more efficient, save all this money, and Taylor set out to prove that management is a true science with laws as exact and as clearly defined as the fundamental principles of engineering. He had an engineering background, and even a cost accounting background. If you think about it, Ed, this idea that management is a true science is the antithesis of this very show.

I mean, this show is the *Soul of Enterprise*, so we're not just talking about the material side of business, we're also saying business enterprise has a *soul*. There's a spirit here and spiritual things can't be measured, so I believe what we are talking about is the antithesis of Taylorism.

Ed: Yes, and he was also a bit nuts, too. As I read up on him, he was 12 years old when he invented something to prick him awake when he would roll over onto his stomach to prevent him from having nightmares. He was a little crazy.

Ron: Yes, at junior high school dances, he would draft charts of girls according to their beauty, and then he would try and divide his time between the pretty ones and the not so pretty ones; and he collected vast amounts of cricket scores. That's probably more exciting than watching cricket itself, so I can't blame him for that. He was a strange duck.

Let me just define Taylorism so people know what we're talking about. It is "The application of scientific methods to the problem of obtaining maximum efficiency in industrial work, or the like." They actually applied this to the homemaker as well — how to be more efficient in the home, and there were all sorts of articles in ladies' magazines. Taylor had a massive impact on the culture during the Progressive Era, from 1890-1920.

He also had many disciples. You want to talk about a strange duck, his disciple Frank Gilbreth, whom they made a movie about called *Cheaper by the Dozen* — not the recent one with Steve Martin — starring Clifton Webb, back in 1950. That was actually based on a book that two of

Gilbreth's kids wrote of the same title. For instance, he was an efficiency expert and he used to shave with two razors because he said, "This saves minutes off the time of shaving," and of course one day he cut himself and that actually cost him more time. This whole cult of efficiency, we are still dealing with the ramifications of it to this day.

Ed: Taylor is the guy who really started all of this. It was his thinking that brought this on. As you said, it was applied in a lot of different places in the <u>Progressive Era</u>. Another one of Taylor's disciples was the guy who invented the <u>Gantt chart</u>, who was huge in the Soviet Union. Those five-year plans really worked out well.

Ron: Lenin was also a disciple of Taylorism. He thought that the new Soviet Union had to really embrace Taylorism to make itself scientific and put it on the map, and also Mussolini was a big fan. In fact, after Taylor died, Mussolini had an audience with Taylor's widow. Taylor's credited with all sorts of things that he didn't really do. Some people say he had something to do with the Holocaust, and this is taking it too far, but there's no doubt that Taylor's ghost still haunts the halls of businesses to this day.

Ed: Absolutely. I was in conversation today with some coworkers on some of these matters, and where it manifests itself today is in terms like 'Scalability,' and certainly efficiency inside an organization.

Efficiency vs. Effectiveness

Ed: Let us set the record straight here. We are not anti-efficiency, are we?

Ron: No. Nobody can be anti-efficiency. However, the problem with this word 'efficiency' is if you attack it, it's like attacking motherhood and apple pie. Go to any business conference, or read a business book, and eventually someone says, "We need to be more efficient." Ed, we should spend some time explaining this, or at least talking about it because you've affectionately labeled this debate that we have at VeraSage "Efficiency Versus Effectiveness." You've labeled this the "Eff'ing Debate."

Let's define this difference. Classically, you hear it put this way, and I just read this definition the other day: "Efficiency is about doing things right, whereas effectiveness is doing the right thing." But that is not true. Efficiency is not doing things right. Efficiency makes no judgment about doing things right. Efficiency is a blind, stupid ratio. It's always a ratio.

Its outputs divided by inputs. It doesn't say anything about doing things right, it's just a measurement. But measurements can obscure reality. They could actually blind us to the truth, and they can actually crowd out judgment.

For instance, I can prove, by measuring, that everybody in the world, on average, has one testicle. Mathematically, I'm right on saying that, but if I believe that as a human being, I'm an idiot.

Ed: Right. This goes to something that is one of the deeper elements that perhaps we'll address in a future show, which is this obsession with measurement of things. I've really come to the conclusion that every measurement is really first a judgment in disguise.

One of the ways that I will demonstrate this is I'll be up in front of an audience and I'll say, "How fast am I moving?" Not fast at all because I'm just standing there. Then I'll say, "What if you took it from the perspective of above the earth?" You would then see that the earth is rotating and I'm moving at a thousand miles per hour. Then, as you get further and further away, the top of the solar system, the earth is going around the sun, and of course our solar system is going around the Milky Way, so it turns out that this is <u>Einstein's theory of relativity</u> applied to business.

The measurement is based on the perceiver, of where you are. That is part of the problem: all too often we just measure stuff because we think we should measure stuff, and no thought is given and no judgment is put into, "Is this the right measurement in the first place?"

Ron: Right. That's such a great example, Ed, and isn't that Kless's Law: all measurements are really judgments in disguise?

Ed: Yes, it's one of the laws that I've coined. You have to then take a step back and ask some questions about that. It's like, "Okay, what am I judging with this measurement?"

Ron: I'm here in Wine Country in Northern California. There's a great saying that the winemakers have around here, which is "It's easier to *count* the bottles than to *describe* the wine." We can count the cost of the grapes and the vines and all of that — all the inputs, the bottles, the corks, etc. — but it says nothing about the value or the quality of the wine.

That takes description. That takes judgment. That takes a refined palate, all of those things. That's what's really important to understand. A measurement is not a judgment, and in a knowledge economy, a judgment is superior to a measurement.

VeraSage Institute

Ed: In all cases, yes. Hey, quickly, Ron, there's a lot of things that we are talking about here that maybe we should fill some folks in on before we undertake things. One, you mentioned earlier the <u>VeraSage Institute</u>, so let's just quickly talk about that one. Would you just give us a brief description of VeraSage.

Ron: <u>VeraSage Institute</u> is a think tank I founded with my two cofounders, <u>Justin Barnett</u> and <u>Dan Morris</u>. Our goal is to teach professionals and business people about the knowledge economy, and how we are now knowledge workers, and how knowledge workers are the opposite of what Taylor studied, which was industrial workers, who worked in steel factories and the like. VeraSage is out there trying to help businesses understand that we live in a knowledge economy and all of the implications of that transformation.

Ed: For the record, I work for a company called <u>Sage</u>. We make and manufacture software. For the longest time, my job has really not been about technology at all, it's really been a business consultant to the folks that implement our software. Over the course of the last two years, I've gotten a chance to get a lot closer to our customers as well, and then also work with the Sage accountants network.

Ron, we came into contact with each other about ten years ago at this point?

Ron: Yes, I believe it was 2004.

Ed: VeraSage has nothing to do with Sage, except the last four letters are the same and, as I like to say, I'm involved with both. That's the only commonality. Tell me the origin of VeraSage, and why it's called "VeraSage." It's a pretty cool thing.

Ron: We had a name consultant come in, and she basically took 'Vera' which is "veracity," and combined it with "sagacity," meaning true wisdom. That's how we got VeraSage. It doesn't have anything to do with Sage, but that's how we came up with the name.

Ed: We should talk about how a lot of the material that we'll be talking about over the course of our show is really based on the thoughts and reflections that you and I have had over the years, and really, the help of the folks who are Fellows of the VeraSage Institute, who constantly challenge our thinking. That's one of the things that you and I love is to be challenged in our thinking.

Ron: Right, because we believe ideas have consequences, and ideas rule the world, and it's really important to study an idea, know its antecedents, but also know its consequences. I believe think tanks are a great model because they operate in the arena of ideas no matter where those ideas come from, so we're always willing to take an idea, turn it around and subject it to our own processes and experiences to see how it comes out. That's what excites me. Ideas excite me.

Ed: Thinking about ideas is clearly very inefficient.

Ron: Yes. But hopefully quite effective.

Ed: That's what we're going to get into in later portions of this program. We're going to contrast the idea of effectiveness and efficiency, and maybe even talk about something that's really cool, the better word that you and I have thrown around, called *efficaciousness*. Efficaciousness. I just love saying it. It's a good word.

Ron: I do, too. There are many more things to say about effectiveness versus efficiency. For example, what if Walt Disney had listened to efficiency experts, and if he did do that, what would have been the consequences?

Snow White and the Four Dwarfs?

Ed: *The Cult of Efficiency is a descendant of the thoroughly discredited Marxian Labor Theory of Value, which has never adequately explained value in a free market, and has no jurisdiction to control the intellectual capital of which the knowledge workers are engaged in creating.*

Happy Independence Day again, Ron.

Ron: You too, Ed. I am loving these quotes that you're springing on everybody. Where are you getting these by the way?

Ed: This is sort of a little inside joke that we have at VeraSage Institute. One thing that we've done a long time ago is to declare independence from the timesheet. I've made minor changes to the VeraSage's <u>Declaration of Independence</u>, and that we are declaring our independence from the tyranny of Taylorism and this cult of efficiency. That's the subject of our show today.

Illustration by <u>Andrew Fyfe</u>

Ed: You were going to tell us a story about Walt Disney and <u>Snow White</u>.

Ron: Here's a great example of why efficiency is not just necessarily doing things right, whereas effectiveness is defined as doing the right thing. If Walt Disney had listened to efficiency experts when he was making *Snow White*, which was known as Disney's folly since everybody thought he'd go broke because nobody wants to sit through a full-length animated feature, he had the studio leveraged to the hilt, he even cashed in his life insurance policies. I mean, everything was riding on this movie, and this was of course in the '30s during the Great Depression.

If he had listened to efficiency experts, they would have come in and seen these animators drawing — there's something like two million hand-drawn animated cells — and they would have said, "Walt, you need to finish this movie. Get it in the can. Get it in theaters. Start earning back some of the money so you can pay off the debts, and all of that." And Ed, your kids would be at home now watching *Snow White and the Four Dwarfs*.

Now certainly, from an output/input ratio, that would have been "more efficient;" however, it wouldn't have been nearly as effective. Disney didn't pursue efficiency, he was after effectiveness, because *The Two Little Pigs* just doesn't have the same ring to it. It's not about efficiency, it's all about effectiveness at the end of the day — *doing the right thing*. There's no right way to do the wrong thing.

Ed: Let's tie this together. The idea here is that knowledge workers are more like artists, in a sense, and I have believed this for years. Business is not a *science*, right? Business is an *art*.

Ron: Absolutely. That's why it was so easy for us to come up with the title of our show, *The Soul of Enterprise*, because we wanted to talk about that artistic nature of business. It's not just something that can be reduced to numbers.

There's No Such Thing as Generic Efficiency

Ed: There's really no such thing as generic efficiency, either. That's a Thomas Sowell quote, isn't it, Ron?

Ron: Yes. First off, was Einstein efficient? How would you even know? By the way, would you even care? From what I understand, when Einstein was stuck, he'd sit in a room, play a violin for hours at a time. Now, this isn't very efficient. He was, however, quite effective.

The other point that needs to be made, Ed, is we can obviously be efficient at doing the wrong things, and there's nothing more useless or more wasteful than being efficient at the wrong thing. That's a very important distinction between these two, but yes, there's no such thing as generic efficiency.

You can't meaningfully define efficiency without regards to purpose, desires, preferences, and how much we're willing to pay for something. For instance, our cars are, for the most part, very inefficient. They are idle 90% of the time, but they are very effective because when you want to go somewhere, you get in and you just go. We make these tradeoffs all the time between these two concepts of efficiency and effectiveness.

Ed: That's changing because we'll soon have driverless cars, and then we won't have to own a second car. That would be a whole other show.

Ron: Absolutely. In a business context, we say there's no such thing as generic efficiency, but this applies to more than business. If you look around the world, ask yourself, "Why do these cities build incredible bridges like the Golden Gate or the Sydney Harbour Bridge?" These aren't very efficient. You could put a military bridge up much quicker, at much cheaper cost, it would carry just as much weight. But a military bridge doesn't appeal to our *souls*. It doesn't have the same impact. That's another really good way to highlight this difference between effectiveness and efficiency.

The other point is that competitive advantage lies with effectiveness. Businesses aren't paid to be efficient. The buggy whip manufacturers were at the apogee of their efficiency, but they were doing the wrong thing by the time the combustion engine came out. The competitive advantages of businesses lie in effectiveness because efficiency can be replicated quite easily by your competition.

Ed: Right. It's about really out-innovating your competition in a lot of cases. I've got a great story about the efficiency/ effectiveness debate, and not meaning anything from a customer perspective. This goes back some 10 years. It's an insurance company, which shall remain nameless.

Somebody said, "Hey, listen. What we really want to do is we want to make sure that we get our life insurance policies in the hands of the customers within 48 hours after they have inked it with the field agent." They implemented all of these systems in place to make sure that this 70-page document was in the hands of the customer within 48 hours.

Here's the problem. If any of you in the audience, or you Ron, have ever gotten your life insurance policy, what did you do with it when you received it?

Ron: I certainly didn't sit there and read it.

Ed: You probably didn't open it right away. It probably sat on the corner of your desk. You're like, "Oh yes. That's the life insurance policy." You weren't thinking, "Oh yes. Let's see. I want to execute on this today," right?

Ron: I hope not.

Ed: That is the last thing you want to do. At best, then it gets stuck in a file some place, because it didn't mean anything to the customer. They're like, "Yippee skippy. We got these to the hands of our customers within 48 hours," but the customers didn't care.

Ron: That's a great example, isn't it, of where we are efficient at doing the wrong thing because it's something that's not adding value to the customer.

Ed: No perception of value to the customer whatsoever, but then, they could make this big claim that, "We have your policy within 48 hours."

Ron: Right, because it's easily measurable and it's just the type of thing that Frederick Taylor would go bonkers over because he can measure it and they can reduce the time and all of that, but if it's meaningless, it's meaningless.

You don't make something effective by making it more efficient. This leads to the other thing, Ed, which you said about knowledge workers being artists and we talked about Einstein and Walt Disney. If you think about efficiency in the knowledge environment when you're dealing with knowledge workers, it takes care of itself because, assuming you're using the latest and greatest technology and all of that, a surgeon is going to be more efficient doing his hundredth surgery than his first two or three. Same with an auditor doing an audit, or pick your trade.

It's kind of the basic human learning curve, or experience curve, which usually takes care of efficiency more than anything else. We just get better because of experience. And doing After Action Reviews will certainly add to both efficiency and effectiveness (see Chapter 2).

Ed: I've got the perfect story for this, and how it doesn't matter to certain people. There's a battle in my house around the dishwasher.

I'm the Frederick Taylor in this story. I am the person who is trying to make sure that we load the dishwasher in the most efficient way. Actually, it's really not so much loading. It's the unloading, so that we can unload it efficiently and make the least number of trips back and forth. Because my job is to unload the dishwasher, and actually load it, too.

That's the deal, but I do a lot of travel, so I'll get home and when I have to unload the dishwasher and it hasn't been loaded to my specifications, it's like, "Oh my God. Here we go." Right?

Here's the really cool part, we now have children. My son, Sean, is eight years old and it's now his job to unload the dishwasher, so now I don't care anymore. Now, I can easily just sit back and say, "You know what? However the dishwasher is loaded is just fine with me," because it's no longer ineffective. It's no longer matters to me.

Ron: It brings up another very interesting point about some of these efficiency experts like Frank Gilbreth and Frederick Taylor. I mean, these guys died young, and a lot of efficiency experts did, and then you sit back and you wonder, "What were they saving all that time for? I just envisioned, in an effective organization, if you unloaded the dishwasher with your son, and maybe you're talking baseball, you would enjoy the time that you were doing that, and the time wouldn't matter, right?"

Ed: That's exactly right. In fact, that's exactly what we did the first couple of times. We were just chatting about things, and I was teaching him where things go, and we even had some conversations as to why they go there, and some of it is because it's not efficient, but it's because it's effective. We know where they are.

Ron: Our mutual mentor, Peter Drucker, wrote one of his classic books, *The Effective Executive*.

Ed: Not *The **Efficient** Executive*.

Ron: Exactly. I just love to point that out because effectiveness is what matters in a business. Businesses aren't paid to be efficient. That is the key point.

The McKinsey Maxim: What You Can Measure You Can Manage

Ed: Nor did Drucker say, "What you can measure, you can manage." He never said it. This is a battle for us, Ron. We know this, because if any of you Google that phrase, "What you can measure you can manage," it will be attributed to Peter Drucker and it makes me crazy.

Ron: He never said it, he never wrote it, and more importantly,

Ed, he didn't believe it. The closest I can tie that Maxim to is the founder of McKinsey & Company, the famous consulting firm, <u>Marvin Bower</u>.

There's a big problem with this bumper sticker concept because again, we get back to this idea that efficiency is a blind, stupid ratio. You could add up Rembrandt's or Picasso's inputs, how much they spent on canvases, paints, etc., but it doesn't tell you anything about the value of their work.

The problem with the McKinsey Maxim, and I say this as somebody who's been reformed on this, is that it's patently false, but I used to believe it in my early career days. Did you as well?

Ed: Yes. It seems to make sense, right? I've even heard the inverse, a cautionary tale, "What you can't measure, you can't manage."

It's this call for, "You've got to be able to measure it." It's not that we shouldn't measure. We can measure stuff. I'm okay with some measurement, but we should understand that it's a judgment in disguise, and is it the right thing that we should be talking about in the first place.

Ron: I really want to dive into this, "What you can measure, you can manage" and falsify it once and for all.

We Can't Change Our Weight by Weighing Ourselves

Ed: *The Cult of Efficiency has a record of multitude of numinous forums and internal bureaucracies and sent hither swarms of officers, nefarious cost accountants, superfluous lean and sick six sigma black belts of various colors, and activity-based costing neophytes to harass our people and eat out their substance.*

That's one of my favorites quotes from our Declaration of Independence. Happy Independence Day, Ron.

Ron: Yes, you too, Ed. I am loving these quotes that you're throwing up.

Ed: Yes. Throwing up, literally.

Ron: Let's get back to the so-called McKinsey Maxim, not the Peter Drucker Maxim.

What you can measure you can manage is another concept, like efficiency, that is just like motherhood or apple pie. You can't attack it. The fact of the matter is, we can't change our weight by having a more accurate scale or weighing ourselves more frequently. Just because we can measure something doesn't at all mean that we can manage it.

In fact, if you think about it, who's ever measured the effectiveness of management? How *do* you measure the effectiveness of management?

You know, we fire CEOs all the time, and managers screw up all the time. What is the measure of an effective manager?

Ed: Usually, it's profit or growth or something like that.

Ron: Humans are messy and we can't be reduced to a simple measurement. There are some big moral hazards in measuring things. My favorite example of this, Ed, is when you sent me that picture of you and Christine and Sean after he had just been born. I wrote you back and said, "Ed, why are you and Christine so happy, your family per capita income just decreased by one third?"

The measurement makes you look poor, and yet, the most joyful day of your life is the birth of a child. The measurement misses the magic of life.

Ed: Right, like when a child is born, per capita GDP goes down, and when a sheep is born, it goes up. That's how messed up economists are. Let's get back to this efficiency/effectiveness debate, and Peter Drucker's book, *People and Performance*, a collection of some his writings. Why don't you tell us a little bit about some of his work there?

Ron: He's got a great line on this. He says, "Efficiency means a focus on costs, but the optimizing approach should focus on effectiveness, and effectiveness focuses on opportunities to produce revenue, to create value, to create markets, to change the economic characteristics of existing products and markets."

This is another thing that we love to cite: *innovation is the antithesis of efficiency*. Frederick Taylor can't go into <u>Google Labs</u> or a pharmaceutical lab with a stopwatch and say, "Hey, you guys. Come up with a brilliant idea by 8:30 am." It doesn't work that way. It's the process of the mind, like you say, Ed, they're artists.

Ed: It's so true. Look, Taylor was just a nasty kind of guy. He said, he was talking about the difference between first class men and the rest, and says that "It's quite as great as the difference between a fine dray horse and donkeys."

This is insulting and yet people apply this stuff and his thinking to knowledge workers every single day out there, and it's killing business. It's killing that soul of enterprise, which is why we're doing this show, because we have to stop it. We have to stop this madness.

Ron: We do. I mean, if you think of companies that you really admire, and we don't have to name our favorites, but I'm sure people have a list of five or more.

Ed: Apple.

Ron: Apple, yes. Apple, Disney, Ritz-Carlton, Nordstrom.

Think about Nordstrom. When you first walked into Nordstrom, I don't know if you remember your first time, but I remember mine. What struck me about it was yes, they have a large selection of shoes, and you can see from one end of the store to the other. They're not your typical rat maze like at Macy's.

But the thing that really struck me was the piano player. Now, there's not an efficiency expert in the world like a

Taylor or Frank Gilbreth who would tell the Nordstrom brothers, "Hey, you guys. Put a piano in your store and hire temperamental musicians." That's not very efficient. If you think about it, it lowers their efficiency ratio of sales per square foot or profit per square foot because that's precious space that could be used for merchandising, and yet, they've decided to put a piano in there to serenade not only their customers, but their team members.

It's another fantastic example of having soul, which means we're going to do things that are aesthetically pleasing for our fellow human beings, and not just because they're efficient.

Ed: It's interesting because I work a lot with entrepreneurs, and it's fascinating to see the growth of an entrepreneurial business, how it starts out with such passion about service to customers or creating something new. Over time, they get professionalized, and they have all of these business consultants who are telling them that they have to start worrying about their efficiency and measuring all this stuff.

What happens, and I've seen this over and over again, is it starts to turn the focus from one that is external, focused on the outside where effectiveness happens, and turns it all inside towards efficiency. We start talking about, "What are the things that we can do to improve sales?" You can't do anything to improve sales. What can you create for customers that improves sales?

That's the questions that people should be asking. Here's my big problem with the Lean Six Sigma ninja turtles. They've claimed that it's in the spirit of the customer, but yet, every time that I've started to scratch the surface with any one of these guys, it all comes down to something that's inside the organization.

Maybe I just don't understand it. I'm willing to say that and suspend that idea, but I've got to tell you the conversations that I've had with these folks have really, really gotten under my skin because it's all about how do we do it better inside the organization.

Ron: So true. Again, they continuously violate Thomas Sowell's line about no such thing as generic efficiency. They would build a military bridge not the Golden Gate because "It's more efficient." This is the problem, and I have encountered the Lean Six Sigma folks constantly, and Lean more than Six Sigma pays lip service to value to the customer, the "voice of the customer," but it's just that — it's lip service. They're much too focused internally, and they don't have a good theory of value because they don't understand that value is in the hearts, minds, and souls of the customer who are external to the enterprise, not the internal processes.

This goes back to companies you admire, like Apple, that understand there's more to buying a computer than just what it can do and its technical specifications. It's how you feel. It's how that brand or that product or service makes you feel. That's a human component that can't be measured.

Ed: Steve Jobs talked about new computers like they were a mistress.

Ron: Yes. One of his marketing people did. The guy was French, so it's understandable.

He said, "If you have an Apple laptop, that's not a computer, that's your mistress." Look at the way people fondle their iPhones, iPads, and their iPods. I mean, these things are aesthetically pleasing to us.

Ed: Yes. You pointed this out to me in airports when you travel, you never see an Apple laptop with stickers all over it.

Ron: No. Nobody ever covers up that logo because they want to tell the world that they think differently, because that's Apple's purpose. Everything we do is because we think differently and challenge the status quo, and that resonates with people.

Ed: Which is why the earbuds on the original iPod, and still to this day, are white. Let's get back to this efficiency topic because it actually does, over time, become dangerous inside an organization.

The moment that an organization starts to worry more about its efficiency as opposed to its outward effectiveness is the moment that it really begins to die. If you had those two things in parallel, you would see that as we think more and more about being effective with our customers, we would think less about efficiency, and if we think more about efficiency, it would decrease our effectiveness.

People get upset with me over that point. They do not think that they're mutually exclusive, but they are. The more you think about efficiency, the less effective you're going to be, and vice versa. The more you think about effectiveness and external value creation, the less you'll worry or care about efficiency.

You taught me a great line: If you have a brain tumor, would you want an efficient surgeon or an effective one?

Ron: Historically, industries that are at the apogee of their efficiency are destined to fall. We call them "Humpty Dumpties." Look at the buggy whips. They were models of efficiency.

There's a great story about Steve Jobs touring an IBM factory that made printers. This was in the early '80s, so you know what was going on in the early '80s, what Jobs had planned. He went through this factory, and it was one of those automated factories that just had robots everywhere and there were like two dogs and three humans, and the humans were there to feed the dogs, and the dogs were there to make sure that the humans didn't touch the robots.

Jobs did this tour, and he was really impressed, and the IBM guys ask, "Steve, what do you think of our factory?" He said, "This is wonderful. It's incredibly efficient. It's too bad you're making the wrong thing." They were making dot-matrix printers.

Now, of course, he made those obsolete with his LaserWriter. A classic example of being very efficient, and yet, here they were about to be made completely irrelevant. If you're efficient at doing something that's irrelevant, or that doesn't add any value, then it's not a very good result.

Systems Thinking

Ed: *We, therefore the hosts of* The Soul of Enterprise *assembled and appealing to the supreme judge of the world for the rectitude of our intentions due in the name and by authority of our listeners solemnly publish and declare that Enterprise is and of right ought to be free and independent from the Tyranny of Taylorism and the Cult of Efficiency.*

Welcome back, folks. Ron, we're going to talk more about efficiency, effectiveness, and you're about to tear something down. Why don't you set that up for us.

Ron: Yes. I'm ready to shoot off some fireworks after that last quote, Ed. Let's talk about this example because this idea that you can look at a business and then break it down into its component parts, whatever that might be — a factory or an office, or what have you.

Any business is an *interdependent system*. This is something I learned from Peter Drucker. You can't just make each part of that interdependent system more efficient and expect to get a more effective whole.

The best way I heard this described was if you are building a world-class sports car. Let's assume you have the mechanical and technical ability to put together the 10,000 parts of a car, and you did your research, and you determined that the best engine in the world is from the Ferrari, and the best handling system is the BMW, and the best brakes are from Porsche, Lamborghini for the interior, and so on.

If you assembled these 10,000 parts you wouldn't have a world-class sports car. You'd have a very expensive pile of junk, because each one of those sports cars is an *interdependent system*. Some parts of it are not efficient, but overall, the whole is effective. That's another problem with efficiency thinking. It breaks things down, and assumes automatically, that if every piece is more efficient, the whole will be more effective.

That's patently false. It's false with the human body, right? The surgeon sometimes has to cut off a pinky to save a hand, or remove an organ, or has to give a treatment that might cause side effects in one area, but that makes you more healthy overall. We have to go back to systems thinking.

Ed: It's interesting because this is a very <u>Newtonian view of the world</u>. It even goes back to the idea that we have this big watch, or this big clock, that's out there. Newton and a lot of the folks of that era did tremendous work from a scientific standpoint. I mean, don't get me wrong, but what we've since learned is that a lot of those things are false and incorrect, especially when applied to business.

Ron: Exactly.

Ed: Business is not Newtonian. It's an entire unified system that as you said, it's completely interdependent, not dependent on certain things. People try to break this stuff down to get little efficiencies here, little efficiencies there, and they in some cases destroy the entire system. It's no accident that when efficiencies tend to go up, customer complaints increase.

Ron: Absolutely. This goes to two more points I'd like to make about this. First, we're not anti-efficiency. <u>Stephen Covey</u> wrote this, "You can be efficient with things, but not people." You have to be effective with people, and, Ed, you have a great line on this from somebody.

Ed: Yes. It's from <u>Pittman Mcgehee</u>, psychologist, who is also a sometime preacher, sometime philosopher, sometime business consultant. He said "The opposite of love is not hate but efficiency."

Ron: I love that line.

Ed: It's so true. One would not describe one's marriage as efficient. If I went downstairs to Christine and said, "I love you, but I really like the fact that we have a very efficient marriage."

Ron: Right. Who wants an efficient marriage? I don't even know what that means. It scares me.

Ed: Right, because it's just crazy, but I'd probably get slapped in the face. It's like, "What do you mean I'm efficient?"

Illustration by Andrew Fyfe

Was Taylor a Fraud?

Ron: That leads us to another point. The thought-provoking book, *The Management Myth*, by Matthew Stewart. It's incredibly provocative, because what Stewart does is take down some of the business gurus of our day, including Peter Drucker. But he really launched some venom at Frederick Taylor. What he said was, "Taylor became famous for the idea of what he was supposed to have achieved, not for what he actually achieved."

One of my favorite lines of Stewart's on Taylor is "One can go grocery shopping with a scientific attitude, but it does not follow that there is a science of grocery shopping." That sums up your line about there's not really a science of business, it's really more of an art.

Ed: Absolutely.

Ron: We, humans, we repel against efficiency. This is why the peacock walks around with this big, beautiful tail, basically telling the female of the species, "See, I can have this big tail which is completely inefficient and still function as a living thing." There's a reason that we're repelled from complete efficiency.

Ed: Yes, we don't like it.

Ron: We inherently trust organizations that have resources to spare.

Back to Matthew Stewart and *The Management Myth* book, he said Taylorism basically was a <u>tautology</u>. An efficient shop is more productive than an inefficient shop. Duh. The fact of the matter is, for all these reasons we've discussed, you can't just be more efficient and expect a more effective whole.

It seems to me, a lot of people who are so focused on efficiency have the Maxim that if you can't manage it, then you should measure it. That can be a big problem as well.

Ed: Absolutely. It gives us the *illusion of control*. It makes us feel better because we can say, "Oh, look, we've got this. We're measuring this." But, it's not real control at all. It's an illusion.

Ron: Right, and even better than effectiveness, why don't we strive to be *efficacious*? I love this word, at least in the context of how pharmaceutical companies use it in terms of drugs. Efficaciousness means *having the power to produce a desired effect*. Viagra is very efficacious.

Ed: Yes. It also has a connotation of achieving the maximum possible benefit, so not just the benefit, but the maximum possible benefit.

Ron: That's what businesses should be striving for, producing that desired effect, of creating value outside of itself, the topic we turn to next.

Supplemental Material

Action January 1, 2001.

The UNANIMOUS DECLARATION of the FOUNDERS of the VeraSage Institute of the PROFESSIONS ASSEMBLED,

WHEN in the Course of Economic Evidence, it becomes necessary for one group of Professionals to dissolve the Traditional Bands which have connected them with another, and to assume among the Powers of the Free Market, the separate and equal Station to which the Laws of Economics entitle them, a decent Respect to the Opinions of the Profession requires that they should declare the causes which impel them to the Separation.

We hold these Truths to be self-evident, that all Value is Subjective, the Customer is sole arbiter of the Value which we in the Professions create, and Price determines Costs, not the opposite—That to secure these Truths, Policies and Procedures are instituted among members of the Profession, and that whenever any Policy becomes destructive of these Principles, it is the Right of the Profession to alter or to abolish it, and to institute new Policies, laying its foundation on such Principles as to them shall seem most likely to effect their Professionalism,

Dignity, Self-respect, and Happiness. Prudence, indeed, will dictate that Traditions long established should not be changed for light and transient Causes; and accordingly all Experience hath shewn, that the Professions are more disposed to suffer than to right themselves by abolishing the Policies and Procedures to which they are accustomed. But when a long Train of Pernicious Effects evinces a Design to reduce them under absolute Despotism, it is their Right, it is their Duty, to throw off such Traditions, and to provide new Procedures for their future Security. Such has been the patient Sufferance of these Founders; and such is now the Necessity which constrains them to alter the former anachronistic Systems of Firm Management. The History of the present Time Accounting is a History of repeated Injuries and Deleterious Effects, all having in direct Object the Establishment of an absolute Tyranny over the Professions. To prove this, let Facts be submitted to a Candid World.

Time Accounting is a descendant of the thoroughly discredited Marxian Labor Theory of Value, which has never adequately explained Value in a Free Market and has no jurisdiction to control the Pricing of Intellectual Capital of which the Professions are engaged in Creating.

Time Accounting has foisted onto the professions the implicit assertion that Time x Rate = Value. This Equation is emphatically false, and is in need of being rejected as without Reason. The Notion that Time is Money is hereby directly rejected.

Time Accounting misaligns the interests of the Professional and the Customer whom it is pledged to Serve.

Time Accounting has focused the Professions solely on hours, not Value, thereby keeping the Professional Mired in Mediocrity at the expense of Entrepreneurial Excellence in the pursuit of opportunities.

Time Accounting places the voluntary transaction risk entirely on the Customer, in direct defiance of the Customer's interests

123

the Professions have pledged to Serve.

Time Accounting fosters a production mentality, not an Entrepreneurial Spirit, thereby hindering the Professions in their attempt to innovate and contribute to the dynamism of the Free Market.

Time Accounting has called together Management and Partners at Places unusual, uncomfortable, and distant from the Professionals and Customers they are bound to Serve, for the sole Purpose of fatiguing them into Compliance with these arbitrary Measures.

Time Accounting creates a subsidy system whereby some Customers will pay for the learning curve of others, and the allocation of Value to any one Customer is completely arbitrary and capricious.

Time Accounting transmits no useful information, as it is definitely not a Critical Success Factor or a Key Predictive Indicator for any member of the Profession, as defined by the Customer whom it is Pledged to Serve.

Time Accounting produces information that is Suspect and subject to inaccuracies and nonfeasance.

Time Accounting has made Owners dependent on Its will alone for the Tenure, Promotion, and the Amount of Payment of Professional Salaries rendered, irrespective of the Value they Create.

Time Accounting has erected a Multitude of new Ominous forms, and internal Bureaucracies, and sent hither Swarms of Officers, Nefarious Cost Accountants, Superfluous Lean and Six-Sigma Belts of various Colors, and Activity Based Costing Neophytes to harass our People, and eat out their Substance, in fifteen minute increments, and sometimes less.

Time Accounting encourages the Hoarding of Hours with no attention paid to the internal efficacious utilization of a Firm's Resources.

Time Accounting has conspired with others to subject us to a Measurement foreign to the Laws of Economics, and unacknowledged by our Self Evident Truths; giving Its Assent to the importance of pretended consequences.

Time Accounting focuses on Efforts, not Results. Customers don't buy efforts, and they don't buy hours, making Time Accounting a measurement of precisely the wrong things.

Time Accounting has become a tool, enhanced by modern technology, already rife with circumstances of Cruelty and Perfidy, scarcely paralleled in any other industry, and totally unworthy of a Proud, and Intellectual Capital based, Profession.

Time Accounting penalizes Technological Advances, as the Professions continue to invest in more and efficient technology, in order to produce more work in less Time, thus lowering Revenue in a Time Accounting Pricing Paradigm.

Time Accounting's Hourly Rates are set by paying attention to competitors, who have no quantifiable interest in the success of any competing enterprise, thereby depriving a Firm's Owners from being compensated for the Value They create.

Time Accounting is a Cost-plus Pricing method that has been thoroughly discredited throughout its inglorious history, and is no longer relevant in a world where wealth is created by Free Minds in Free Markets. It is not the Customer's duty to provide the Professions with a Desirable Net Income; it is the duty of the Professions to Provide a Service that is so good, the Customer Dutifully Pays a Profit in Recognition of what was done for them. Profit is a Lagging Indicator, at best, and is a Result of a Job well done, an Applause. In a Free Market, costs do not determine price, rather, price determines costs and value determines price.

Time Accounting defies the imperative rule of private, Free Market

Transactions; that is, the Price is known to the Customer before they purchase a product or service. The Professions Defy this well-known Law at their Own Peril.

Time Accounting does not Differentiate one firm in the Profession from another. Rather, it transforms the Crown Jewels of any one Firm—the human and social capital, experience, wisdom, professional judgment and intellect—into one completely arbitrary Hourly Rate, viewed as a Commodity by the Public.

Time Accounting imposes an arbitrary ceiling on the Income Potential of the Professions, as there is only a fixed quantity of hours in any given day, week, month, year or life. This ceiling has been imposed by Time Accounting, not the Public the Professions are Pledged to Serve.

Time Accounting diminishes the Quality of Life of the Professional, by viciously segregating His or Her Time into Billable and Non Billable segments. Rather than being a device for tracking the Inventory of Time, Time Accounting has become the Inventory.

In every stage of these Oppressions we have Petitioned, Pleaded and Exhorted the Profession's Leaders and Consultants for Redress in the most humble Terms: Our repeated Petitions have been answered only by repeated Injury and Ridicule. A Master, whose Character is thus marked by every act which may define a Tyrant, is unfit to be the arbitrary Ruler of a free Profession in a Free Market.

Nor have we been wanting in Attentions to Leaders and Consultants of the Profession around the world. We have warned them from Time to Time of Attempts by their anachronistic Practices to extend an unwarrantable Jurisdiction over us. We have reminded them of the Circumstances of our Emigration and Conception of a radical business model for Professional Firms. We have appealed to their native Justice and Magnanimity, and we have conjured them by the Ties of our common Knowledge and Interests to disavow these Usurpations, which, would inevitably interrupt our Connections and Correspondence and hinder the Future of the Professions. They too have been deaf to the Voice of Justice, Economics, and of Consanguinity. We must, therefore, acquiesce in the Necessity, which denounces our Separation, and hold them, as we hold the rest of the Professions, wrong in the Marketplace of Ideas.

We, therefore, the Representatives of VeraSage Institute, in GENERAL CONGRESS, Assembled, appealing to the Supreme Judge of the World for the Rectitude of our Intentions, do, in the Name, and by Authority of the good People of this Institute, solemnly Publish and Declare, That this Institute is, and of Right ought to be, FREE AND INDEPENDENT FROM THE TYRANNY OF TIME; that it is absolved from all Allegiance to the Past Traditions as they relate to Time Accounting, and that all Measurements and Procedures between them are and ought to be totally dissolved; and that as FREE AND INDEPENDENT PROFESSIONALS, they have full Power to Price on Purpose and for Value, levy Ideas in the Free Market, contract Alliances, establish Commerce, engage in Capitalist Acts between Consenting Adults, and to do all other Acts and Thoughts which INDEPENDENT PROFESSIONALS may of right do. And for the support of this Declaration, with a firm Reliance on the Protection of divine Providence, we mutually pledge to each other our Lives, our Fortunes, our Energies, and our sacred Honor.

Signed by Order *and in* BEHALF *of* VeraSage Institute,

RONALD J. BAKER, California
JUSTIN H. BARNETT, California
DANIEL D. MORRIS, California
ED KLESS, Texas

Miscellaneous

Book Review: *Frederick Taylor: The One Best Way*
Book Review: *The Management Myth*

Blog post: <u>Efficiency vs. Effectiveness</u>
Blog post: <u>Pigs, Productivity, and Purpose</u>
LinkedIn Blog post: <u>Stop Worrying About Efficiency</u>
Sign the VeraSage Institute <u>Declaration of Independence</u>

Part 3 — A Theory of Everything

Chapter 4: <u>The First Law of Marketing: All Value is Subjective</u>

"Value is…nothing inherent in goods, no property of them. Value is a judgment economizing men make about the importance of the goods at their disposal for the maintenance of their lives and well-being. Hence value does not exist outside the consciousness of men…[T]he value of goods…is entirely subjective in nature."
— Carl Menger, <u>*Principles of Economics*</u>

Ron: Ed, why are diamonds more expensive than water?

Ed: It's a great question.

Ron: After all, you can live without diamonds, but you can't live more than a few days without water.

This is known as the diamond-water paradox. It's something that confounded <u>Adam Smith</u>. He even wrote about it in his famous book, <u>*The Wealth of Nations*</u>, which was published in 1776, the same year that we declared our independence.

How do you think Adam Smith solved this paradox?

Ed: I don't think he ever really solved it. He just skirted around it and said, "I really can't quite explain it, so I'm going to give you a partial theory and say that it might be labor or scarcity.

Ron: He didn't solve it. The closest he got for a theory was that, "Diamonds are more scarce than water."

After all, water covers roughly 71% or so of the earth's surface. If you were to ask a lot of business people today, they still tend to say that diamonds are more valuable than water because they are scarcer.

Ed: Yes.

Ron: Yet, we know that scarcity doesn't explain value. After all, if it did, then those drawings on your refrigerator, Ed, by your kids would be Picasso's. They're one of a kind.

The Labor Theory of Value

Ron: This is what I find so interesting about the history of economic ideas. These ideas don't just drop out of the sky, they come from real humans based upon our experience, how we interact, how we barter, how we exchange, and how we buy things. Therefore, it's worth exploring the different theories of value that came through the ages.

We always talk about the physiocrats, Ed, the group of economists from France who thought that the only value was that which was extracted from the land.

Ed: Right. If you were a shepherd, you're okay, but if you sheared the sheep and then knitted a wooly hat, you are exploiting the shepherd.

Ron: That's obviously bonkers. Then, of course, the most famous theory came from <u>Karl Marx</u>. Of course, this theory can be traced all the way back to <u>Aristotle</u> and even <u>St. Thomas Aquinas</u>. It's known today as the <u>Labor Theory of Value</u>, and this is what Adam Smith thought as well: that the more labor that goes into a commodity — a good or a service — the more valuable it is to the consumer.

When you subject this to the real world, it fails to explain how you and I buy things.

Ed: No question. Customers don't care about your costs or your inputs. I beg people when I talk to them to, please, don't try to justify your price by talking about your costs to your customer because they don't care. I mean, none of us walks into a hotel and thinks, "I hope the Hilton has their cost structure figured correctly so they make a profit on me."

We have booked the hotel room because we need it, because we value it, and we got a price for it, but you don't care about the cost. Yet businesses try to do this all the time and major businesses, the airlines especially, with their fuel surcharges. They even will put out press releases about, "The costs have gone up, so therefore we have to adjust our prices upwards." It's just insane.

Ron: It is. The way I like to think about this is it's like when a loved one or a friend has a baby. You want to see the baby. You don't want to hear about the labor pains. Focusing on the cost is the labor pains, and the customer doesn't care about that. They care about the baby, the result, the outcomes, the value.

The interesting thing about your point about justifying price based upon cost is this has been true throughout history. If you go back to medieval English, the word "Acre" is the amount of land that a team of oxen could plough in a morning. We've always equated labor, and especially time, with money whether you trace it back to Benjamin Franklin's line "time is money," or just the idea that effort and labor are equated to value.

It's false. It's worth explaining that not only did Adam Smith, who was a genius in explaining the free market system, get this wrong, but so did David Ricardo, another famous economist who gave us the Law of Comparative Advantage.

Ricardo was actually lying on his deathbed and pondering the conundrum of why a bottle of wine becomes more valuable with age when no more labor went into it.

Ed: Right, or why a tree that grew to be a mighty oak with only two pence of labor put into it was then worth a hundred pounds once it was cut up.

The Marginalist Revolution of 1871

Ron: Luckily, a group of economists did come along and falsified the Labor Theory of Value. One of my favorite examples of this is if the Labor Theory of Value were true, then a rock found next to a diamond in a mine should be of equal value because it took the miners just as much labor to find and extract the rock as it did the diamond, and yet, I don't see jewelry stores with rocks in their display cases.

Ed: It's even interesting that there's a biblical story that talked about the Parable of the Laborers in the vineyard and how the vineyard owner hired some laborers in the morning, some at noon, and then some later in the day, and then paid them all the same wage. The folks who were hired in the morning were ticked. They were not happy with the price.

The vineyard owner says, "Who are you to question the authority of the owner?" There's also an economic explanation for that if you really think about it, not that I believe the Bible is an economics textbook, but that you could say, "Maybe the vineyard owner thought there was going to be a frost that night, and the grapes that were harvested later in the day were of more value because otherwise, they were going to be ruined."

Ron: Right. You know what? I can think of a lot of scenarios where it makes perfect sense, or just the fact that he was happy to get the extra help that late in the day.

The thing about the Labor Theory of Value that is really wrong is Karl Marx ignored the consumer, because if you think about it...

Ed: He hated consumers, Ron. That's why.

Ron: Yes, and he hated profit too. If you think about it, if the Labor Theory of Value is right, then today maybe for lunch or dinner, you'll have pizza. Your tenth slice should be just as valuable as your first or second. Your tenth shot of tequila should be just as valuable because it took the same amount of labor to produce, but obviously, there's a law of diminishing returns here for us humans. The more we consume of something, the less valuable it becomes. That's the big hole in the Labor Theory of Value — it ignores the consumer.

Ed: Why do you think it's so pervasive today? Because it just seems to makes sense, is that why? If you don't look at it deeply, it just makes sense.

Ron: There is a visceral and intuitive reasoning behind it. After all, if I'm making this elaborate piece of furniture, or a Stradivarius violin, there's a lot of skill and craftsmanship involved, it will probably command a higher price.

The problem with it is that there is no correlation between labor time and value. I could spend decades of my life writing a book that doesn't sell. What can I say, that the world owes me a living because I spent all this time? It's obviously false, but there is a certain intuitive sense to it, isn't there?

Ed: Yes, and didn't Marx actually think that his family should support him because he was doing important work?

Ron: Absolutely. The guy was a real pauper. He never repaid his debts, and his mom had a great line about him, "I wish Karl would spend more time creating some capital rather than just writing about it."

Even Adam Smith said that if it cost twice the labor to kill a beaver as it does to kill a deer, obviously the one beaver should exchange for two deer. It might make intuitive sense, but it's absolutely wrong because, again, it ignores the consumer.

Ed: Right, who is the ultimate arbiter of value.

Ron: The consumer doesn't care about a business's costs or efforts, they don't even care about how much profit a business makes; they really care about the value to them. I guess this leads us to our first law of marketing, and it's really not about the value of value. We should more accurately say it's actually the value of having the correct theory of value.

And that correct theory is that *all value is subjective*.

Ed: It just can't be, Ron. It just can't be. It's just too easy.

Ron: I know. Then, people say to us, "There can never be an absolute so you can never use all," but I do want to make that point that all value is subjective. It is like beauty. It's in the eye of the beholder. If it wasn't true, Ed, then if you and I went to a movie, we should like it equally well because, after all, it took the same amount of labor to produce that movie for both of us to be able to watch it, and yet, I might come out of the movie hating it while you loved it.

Ed: Ron, we've talked about the Labor Theory of Value, and then we have suggested that there is this other theory of value, the Subjective Theory of Value, and this isn't just you and I coming up with this. This was put forward by a group of economists in the late 1800s. They're called "The Marginalists," right?

Ron: Yes, and thank heavens for these folks because these three guys basically came up with this theory of subjective value separately. It was William Stanley Jevons from Great Britain, Leon Walras from France, and Carl Menger from Austria.

They first falsified Marx's Labor Theory of Value, citing some of the same examples that we just talked about, and then they posited that all value is subjective. Again, like beauty, it's in the eye of the beholder. What they also said was that *there's no such thing as intrinsic value*. Value is not intrinsic to goods. We only use goods or resources because they serve some purpose for us.

If you think about it, the only thing on this planet that has

135

intrinsic value from an economic standpoint would be human life, but products and services don't have intrinsic value. We used to use whale oil, and we don't use it anymore because we found better substitutes. If we ever find a better substitute for oil, we won't use that anymore either, so there is no such thing as intrinsic value, or even a natural resource.

Ed: I want to leverage off that point because this is a huge, huge challenge for most folks in business. Business people all of the time make the same category mistake when they think that their stuff, whatever it is — their product, service, or knowledge — has some kind of objective value that you can say, "This is what it's worth, and therefore it has value."

They're making the same category mistake. I find this thinking fascinating because it is so endemic in business thinking, i.e., that our stuff must have value because we say it does, or because it cost us time and money to produce.

Ron: I'm always challenged by somebody about gold. They say, "Gold has intrinsic value." If we found out tomorrow that gold was a carcinogenic, what would its value be? Gold doesn't have intrinsic value. It only has value because people believe it does. It's a spiritual source of value, not a physical source.

This is another reason that the show is called *The Soul of Enterprise* because we're not just trying to explain the material here, we're also trying to explain the spiritual, and money, gold, and value are all spiritual.

Ed: Wait! Money is spiritual, Ron?

Ron: Yes, it absolutely is. I know we have little numbers printed on it, and that makes it look objective, but the only reason you take a five-dollar bill from me is because you trust that it's worth five dollars when you go to buy something else.

Ed: Yes. There's a great story, I believe Milton Friedman tells it

136

in his book, *Money Mischief*, about the Micronesian Island of Yap, somewhere in the Pacific. The deal is that the money in this society was due to the limestone tavern that they found at this other island, and they brought these huge rocks over from this other island. They've been there hundreds of years, and that was then considered to be the value for the society. They're all over the place.

They're in front of people's houses, they're in the middle of the village, and the way that it works is to make a payment, you just say to someone, "Okay. This rock here is not mine anymore. It's yours." It's then just known throughout the village "Okay. The big one at the corner of fifth and Lamar, that's Fred's now," and everybody just agrees.

In fact, it's to the point where there's a legend of one of these rocks getting sunk when they were transporting it. There was a storm that arose just before they landed, and it's a couple of hundred yards off shore, and it's still agreed that this belongs to the richest family on the island. It just happens to be at the bottom of the ocean. People think that this is crazy, but that's the same thing that money is in our society, right?

My dad was a Latin teacher. *Fiat* means *So it is*.

Ron: It's a great story. Two other points about the Labor Theory of Value contrasted with the Subjective Theory of Value. First, Karl Marx would say that pearls have value because people spend labor diving for them, whereas the marginalist economists who posited the *Subjective Theory* would say, "No, no. People dive for pearls because other people find them valuable."

If I find a pearl walking down the street, I'm going to be able to sell it for the same amount as if I work five weeks to find one, right? It's not the inputs that matter, it's the output, and it's the value to the consumer.

Second, when you buy something as a consumer — a latte

at Starbucks — you're only doing it because it's worth more to you than what you're paying. One of the problems with accounting, and the whole debits equals credits worldview, is in the real world debits don't equal credits. Not only, hopefully, does Starbucks make a profit on that transaction, but the customer does as well, because exchange is based on unequal perceptions of value.

It's not that that cup of coffee is worth four dollars to you, it has to be worth *more* than four dollars to you, otherwise, you wouldn't have bought it. But that difference doesn't get booked on the consumer's home accounting system.

Ed: Right, but not necessarily monetarily, right? That gets into the whole idea of money in a sense is spiritual because yes, you're trading this four dollars for it, but there is the good feelings, there is the pleasure of sipping the hot cup of coffee that is more valuable to you than the four dollars, and money is really just this medium of exchange, but it's the trade where the value is actually created on both sides. It's clear to people who are doing accounting that, "Okay. We have all of our revenue minus our cost as our profit," but what they don't see is the fact that, "It's actually on the consumer side where we are creating more value than the price."

This is referred to in a lot of cases as that weird "<u>Double Thank You</u>" <u>moment</u>, when you go into some place and buy something and you say "Thank you" to the clerk, and they say "Thank you" back.

Ron: Right. That's a very interesting economic and social phenomenon.

Ed: Why is that? Because we both wanted this trade to happen. Now, this is not to say that all trades are always creating value on both sides, right? There's such thing as buyer's remorse, there are sometimes when people are forced into having to buy something, there are times when there isn't necessarily value created, and especially when prices are being manipulated in some way.

Ron: Sure. Yet the great majority of transactions happen because I value whatever it is I'm buying more than the money I'm giving up.

Ed: One of the things that I've talked about with people is sometimes they think that they're getting exploited by their employer. They think, "The stuff that I'm doing is way more valuable to my employer than the amount that I get paid." I'm like, "Yes."

That's the way it's supposed to work. You are working whether it's providing in a sense your labor, but also, and importantly your knowledge, and they want it more than they want the salary that they pay you, otherwise you wouldn't have a job.

Ron: Right, it's a great point. A couple of months ago, I was at San Francisco Airport boarding an airplane. You would not believe this conversation two women were having right in front of me. You know how you can just overhear when you're standing right behind somebody in line, getting ready to board a plane. They were talking about this word, "value."

They were saying, "It's the biggest buzz word. The company is using it, but we don't know what it is. How do you measure value? How do you quantify value?" And they went on and on. I couldn't contain myself anymore, so I had to butt in and say, "I couldn't help overhearing you ladies talk about value. I've written a few books on this." I said, "I'd love to have a discussion with you on it," and they asked me real quick as we were walking down the jetway, "Give us a definition of value."

I said, "Think about it this way. Let's say you're in the desert and you're dehydrated and you're about to die. What would a bottle of water be worth to you? It'd be priceless because it would save your life? Now, imagine you're home washing the dog or dishes with the same quantity of water. Now, what's that water worth to you? Obviously a lot less. If you're flooded in your basement with water, now what's it worth to you? Obviously negative, since you have to pay somebody to come out and pump it out."

I said, "Notice in each of those examples that we didn't change at all the physical characteristics of the product. It's still H_2O. In fact, if you think about it even from a cost accounting perspective, the cost of getting that water to those three locations doesn't change that much, certainly not enough to drive it from infinite value to negative value. What changed is the context you're in and the job you're trying to perform. In other words, the subjective perception of value to you, the consumer.

Ed: How did they feel about that, Ron?

Ron: They thought it was great. By the way, one of the books I wrote about this is _Pricing On Purpose: Creating and Capturing Value_. I was actually sitting across the aisle from one of the ladies and she actually bought my book on the plane and started reading it. They really understood with that example that, "Yes, that makes complete sense, that it depends on my context what something is worth to me, not the cost of getting it to me."

Ed: Exactly. Just on that water example, take a look at Penn & Teller's video where they created a water steward at a restaurant and filled up the bottles with regular hose water, but yet the perception of value is much higher because of the context and how it's presented, and the people actually say, "This tastes so much better."

Ron: Yes, and the range of prices they charge for it is absolutely stunning.

The Far Niente Story

Ed: Ron, one of the most fantastic stories I've ever heard you tell is about a favorite winery of yours called <u>Far Niente</u>. Just to set this up, Far Niente is a winery in Napa Valley and they make a particular cabernet sauvignon that you absolutely love.

By the way, Far Niente is Italian for *Do Nothing*, which is just the absolute perfect name for a winery.

Ron: Like you said, I particularly enjoy one particular vintage of cabernet that they make. It's a reserve and estate bottled, it's limited and sells for about $150 more than their typical cabernet. I buy it for people for special occasions, wedding anniversaries, 50th Birthdays, things like that, and everybody who imbibes has really, really enjoyed it. It makes you feel good.

Finally, I got to tour this winery several years ago. The tour guide takes us down into this barrel room and he starts explaining that, "This is where we bottle this particular vintage." Now it's really important to understand that I had been buying this particular vintage for about seven years before I took the tour, long before I knew anything about how they made this wine.

He is explaining to us how they can't bottle this wine automatically using their bottling machines. He says, "We have to hire people to come down here, stand at the barrels and fill the bottles by hand, and then cork it manually and other special handling." He turned around to the group, and there were about 12 of us, and he said, "And that's why this wine is more expensive." Everybody nodded their head and moved on, just like you said about "Businesses justify higher prices because of higher costs." Everybody just accepted it, because it aligns with our perception of fairness.

141

I didn't have the heart to give this guy an economics lesson and ruin the tour, but he's wrong. He's got the cause and effect completely backwards. That wine is not worth more to me because they bottled it by hand. In fact, I had no idea they bottled it by hand or that it cost more to make, nor do I care. I still don't care, and I know all about it, because to me, that's the labor pains and not the baby.

What was missing was the reason Far Niente is willing to incur those additional labor costs is because people like me value the wine so much that I'm willing to pay a price that's high enough to cover those additional costs. The chain works exactly the opposite of what he said on the tour.

Ed: Right, and we've pointed this out on a number of educational sessions that we teach. So many people think it's costs that drive price, then price that drives value, and then that value is then justified to the customer. I remember the first time that you and I talked about this and the epiphany that I had. I said, "But where does the customer come in that chain?" Dead last.

Ron: Right.

Ed: They're the last ones that are considered, which is exactly why Marx got it wrong. He didn't consider the customer in this theory, yet in reality they actually came first as the ultimate arbiters of value. Yet, business people today still say, "The customer comes first. The customer comes first."

Okay. Let's live that. If the customer comes first, then they are the soul arbiter of value, the value then will determine what the price is, and the price then justifies the cost, which is the lesson of the Far Niente story, right? Price justifies costs, it doesn't come from them. And value justifies price.

The challenge of course is that there are lots and lots of systems out there that embrace cost-plus pricing that ask, "How are you going to price this item?" It's a percent mark up.

Ron: Right. Here's how it looks in graphical form:

Cost-Plus Pricing — Labor Theory of Value

Product → Cost → Price → Value → Customers

Value-Based Pricing — Subjective Theory of Value

Customers → Value → Price → Cost → Product

Why Are Diamonds More Expensive Than Water?

Ed: It leads us to believe that it's based on marking up all of our costs. Apple doesn't do anything that way. Coming back to this idea of value, Ron, let me ask you the question, and now we need to answer it. Why are diamonds more valuable than water?

Ron: Obviously, there is a subjective value component. It's also part two of the marginalist explanation of value. It's actually known as Gossen's Law, this German economist by the name of Hermann Heinrich Gossen who basically said, "The market price is always determined by what the last unit of a product is worth to people."

Obviously, the first bottle of water that's going to save your life when you're dehydrated in the desert is going to be priceless, but as you consume more and start washing the dog, then your car, and then hose down the driveway, those last gallons at the margin are going to be worth a lot less, and the market price tends to flow to the last marginal value used; but the marginal value of a second diamond, even if you're Liz Taylor, is pretty high.

Illustration by <u>Andrew Fyfe</u>

Ed: Tie this in because the objection that I usually get when talking to folks about this is, and we haven't talked about this at all, is what about supply and demand?

Ron: Yes, and we will deal with that in Chapter 5. Let's go back to this idea of the marginal unit, the next one. That's what the margin means, the next one.

Take as an example — and I don't even think you can find these much anymore — <u>the old newspaper racks</u>. Remember those that sold *The New York Times*, maybe you put in eight quarters or whatever. Notice that *The New York Times* didn't design those racks to only pull out one paper at a time.

You could reach in there and theoretically take all the papers you wanted, but yet, if there was a Coke machine nearby that rack, it's got this elaborate <u>Rube Goldberg mechanism</u> to make sure only one Coke dispenses. Why is that?

A sociologist, or a criminologist, looking at this might say, "Obviously, *New York Time* readers are more honest than Coke drinkers." That's not a very good theory.

The theory of marginalism explains this better because the second *New York Times* isn't worth that much, right? Whereas the second Coke, or third or fourth, can be stored and enjoyed later. That's why Coke will spend more money to make sure people only get one at a time, and that's why water is so much cheaper than diamonds, because, if you think about it, if water companies knew that you are in the desert, of course they would charge you a higher price.

They do this if you think about bottled water, we pay more for bottled water than we do for gas.

Ed: In some cases, yes. Absolutely. If you're buying it out at a ball field or worse, the U.S. Tennis Open, where I hear water is just incredibly expensive, and you're not even allowed to bring it in, you're going to pay more for it than you are for gasoline.

Ron: Of course, it's because it's convenient. You can take water with you when you ride your bike or jog or whatever, and so we're paying for that convenience, but it's really the idea that the market price tends to gravitate to that last marginal use. It's a tendency, not a rule. And it should be said municipal water from our taps is not "free," or cheap. We pay enormous taxes for it.

Back to your other point, Ed, about the Far Niente story and how it illustrates that it's value that determines the price I was willing to pay for that wine, and it was at a higher price I was willing to pay because the value is so great to me that they were able as a winery to hire those additional laborers and still make a profit. Think about if this theory wasn't true.

If this wasn't true — if our cause and effect here, the way we are explaining it wasn't true — then why would any

145

business go bankrupt? It's not that difficult to put a price above your costs that include some profit, right? The reason businesses go bankrupt is because they make things that other people don't value.

Ed: Yes. My six-year-old daughter could figure out a way to put a price above her costs. She understands the differences between numbers and that one number is higher than another number.

Ron: It's not that difficult, but businesses fail because they don't produce things that customers value enough to cover their costs. I just read the other day that General Motors (GM) is recalling 17 times more cars than they sold this year?

Ed: That whole GM story is absolutely incredible. Unfortunately, GM has become a pension fund that happens to make cars.

Ron: It's a classic example of cost-plus pricing. GM is saying, "Hey, because we have costs and because our shareholders expect some profit, therefore, Mr. Customer, you have to cover our costs even if we produce crap." That's not the way the real world works.

Ed: As incredible as it sounds, it was in 2009 or 2010, GM and Toyota produced within 500 cars of one another in the United States. Yet, Toyota did it at a profit and GM did it at a loss.

Ron: What's interesting about Toyota is it does not have a standard cost accounting system. Now, as a former cost accountant, that absolutely blew my mind. This is well documented in a great book by H. Thomas Johnson — a professor of accounting — _Profit Beyond Measure_.

Toyota understands that what drives the price of their cars is the perception of value to the customer. So before they even build a car, they know what the price is going to be, and then their job is to incur costs less than that price to make an adequate profit.

Ed: Tell the story of the executive at Ford Motor Company who back in the day actually understood that chain of causation.

A Tale of Two Automobiles

Ron: It's what I call the Tale of Two Automobiles; it is a great story.

In the 1950s, after soldiers were returning from World War II, there was a lot of pent-up demand for consumer durables; they had been over in Europe, they had obviously seen some sports cars, and a particular automobile company thought the market was right for a sports car, so they gave their engineers carte blanche, like a Skunkworks project: "Hey, you guys. Build the car of your dreams, high performance, sexy, sporty, all of that." And these engineers went to town on this car, and it was introduced in 1953 at a retail price of $3,490.

There's a Harvard Business Review case study, and you can see how they priced this car. They added up all the cost of production, materials, labor, etc. They added a certain amount of profit per car, and then of course they projected how many units they thought they were going to sell, and so it was a traditional cost-plus pricing formula.

The car bombed in its first year, only selling 400 units, so they lost money. In 1955, it turned around, they started making money on it, and this car is still made to this day. As this car was getting out there and was getting rave reviews and people really liked it, another executive at a different automobile company would talk to people, and they'd come up to him and they'd say, "We really love that sports car." He said, "Why aren't you driving one?" "It's too expensive." He started asking people, "What would you like in a sports car? What features?" And they would tell him.

He also asked, "What would that be worth to you?" He

came up with a target price of $2,500. Now, it obviously had to be less than this other car, otherwise they would have just went and bought that one.

The important part is how he went back to his engineers and asked, "Can you make this car with these features that we can sell at this price at a profit we can live with?" The engineers scratched their heads because this isn't how automobiles were made in the post-World War II era — it was a more "build it and they will come" attitude. This is how we got the big fins on automobiles, anything they built they could sell.

The engineers figured it out and the car was released in 1964. It actually came in under its target price of $2,500. It retailed at $2,390, and in the first two years, it made $1.1 billion in *profit* for this company.

Now, just to put that in context, this other car from 1953 up to 2010 is about one-third of that $1.1 billion in profit. This illustrates really well the idea of starting with value to the customer and working backwards. Of course the two cars I'm talking about are the Corvette, which is still being made, and the Mustang, which is also still being made; in fact, it's having its 50th anniversary this year [2014].

I just love that story because what it illustrates is that pricing for value doesn't necessarily always mean a higher price. The Mustang was cheaper.

Ed: Yes, and the Ford executive was a fellow by the name of Lee Iacocca.

Ron: He wrote about the story in his first autobiography, and the Mustang was an enormous success and everybody wanted to take credit for it — the classic line that "A failure is an orphan, but success has many different fathers or many different mothers," as they say.

That's, by the way, how Toyota builds cars, and in fact all the Japanese automakers build cars with that same process.

They start with value to the customer. That determines the price, and then they work backwards to engineer the cost.

Ed: It's called target costing, right Ron?

Ron: Yes, I wrote a <u>review</u> on a <u>book</u> — _<u>Target Cost Management</u>_ by <u>Jim Rains</u> — about this concept. The Japanese have been using it for quite a long time. They moved a long time ago away from cost-plus pricing. Also, companies in the technology sector utilize it, such as Apple, software companies, etc.

Ed: Absolutely, and we at Sage do use it. It's a great methodology, because it is the antithesis of what Marx was talking about, because it puts the customer first in the value chain. That's really the big difference.

Ron: I also have an ethical problem with cost-plus pricing. It's as if the world owes us a living because we've incurred all these costs, we have overhead, we have profit desires, and therefore, Mr. and Mrs. Consumer, you have to pay a price that covers all my costs even if I produce something that's of no value. It's almost an entitlement mentality.

Ed: Yes, and you and I have talked about this. We work primarily with people in what we call the professional service sector, but it can also be called The Knowledge Worker Economy. They think they're in the service sector, and in many cases, they'll use the same ideas like, "But I worked on that for ten hours," so therefore, it must have value to the customer."

The reality is is that they are taking a theory of value, the Labor Theory of Value, primarily put forward and codified best by Karl Marx, who thought that profit was evil, and trying to build profit into the system. It completely makes no sense. In a sense, professionals who bill by the hour are practicing Marxists. That's the reality.

Ron: Absolutely. I know people get upset with that, but that's where this idea comes from. Again, these theories don't just drop out of the sky, they came from somewhere. If you've ever been charged by the hour from your plumber, or your attorney, or your accountant, it's the Labor Theory of Value in action. Just because they spent more time, it should be worth more to you. That's just patently absurd.

Ed: We are going to bring this together in the next chapter. There's the first law of marketing, and so it follows that there must be at least a second law of marketing.

Ron: Right. The first law is that all value is subjective, and you can think of that as the first law of marketing. Now, to bring supply and demand into it, to bring competition into this, you may actually pay a lot less for something that you value dearly, and therefore earn a large profit as a buyer. That's the second law of marketing, which is *all prices are contextual*.

Ed, it's even broader than that, isn't it? All decisions are contextual, and not just about pricing. We weigh one thing against another, or make trade-offs as economists say.

Ed: Yes. It's a fascinating topic that we will explore next.

Supplemental Material

LinkedIn Blog post: <u>A Tale of Two Theories</u>, which contrasts the Labor Theory of Value with the Subjective Theory of Value.

LinkedIn Blog post: <u>The First Law of Marketing: All Value is Subjective</u>, which also explains the tale of two automobiles, and the problems with cost-plus pricing, which Ron and Ed discussed.

LinkedIn Blog post: <u>Who's in Charge of Value</u>, which explains the idea of appointing a Chief Value Officer and Value Council in your company.

LinkedIn Blog post: <u>Car Guys vs. Bean Counters</u>. This is Ron's book review of the book by Bob Lutz, a diagnostic book on the demise of General Motors: <u>Car Guys vs. Bean Counters: The Battle for the Soul of American Business</u>. Since we discussed the problems General Motors is currently having, this book provides more detail on why it is having these issues.

Chapter 5: <u>The Second Law of Marketing: All Prices are Contextual</u>

The truth is, it's actually more fair to treat different customers differently. A customer who invests more in your firm is certainly owed a greater level of service and attention, and by treating customers individually the enterprise can usually raise the general level of service for nearly all customers. Customers don't want to be treated equally. They want to be treated individually...Any company that treats a customer the same as "everybody" is treating that customer like nobody.

— Don Peppers and Martha Rogers
<u>*Enterprise One to One: Tools for Competing in the Interactive Age*</u>

Ed: Ron, do you want to buy my unicorn?

Ron: Well, I've never bought one before so give me some context.

Ed: Exactly. There in a nutshell sums up our second law of marketing, which is, *All prices are contextual*. In the last chapter we discussed the first law of marketing, which is, *All value is subjective*, and we talked about a lot of dead economists and why some were right, and others were wrong, and our evolution in understanding what value is.

This second law completes what we believe is a universal theory of everything in business, which is, *All value is subjective and all prices are contextual*, and as you say it's even bigger than that, isn't it? It is actually all decisions are contextual.

Ron: Definitely. We always compare one thing to another. What I like about these two laws of marketing is when you combine them, it can help any business not only create more value, help them communicate more value, but also capture more of that value from their customers with better pricing strategies.

Ed: It's interesting because this week I received an email from Amazon announcing it now has Kindle Unlimited, which allows people to read any Kindle, but, well, it's not that easy upon further review. I did find out that <u>Kindle Unlimited</u> is actually limited. There are some limitations.

Long and short is that for $9.99 a month, Amazon will let you look at 600,000 titles and stream audio books. You then have to fill in the context for that, right? You're trying to figure out, "Well, how many books do I buy a month? Will the books that I want be on the list?" All right, it's an example of where all prices are contextual and then, if it were truly unlimited, it might be even harder to put a price on it, wouldn't it?

Ron: It would. By saying unlimited, they're actually making it difficult for me to compare it to something else. If they were to put an artificial limit on it, say 500 books, or 200, or whatever, that might be more understandable, at least it would give me some context to make a comparison.

Ed: Yes, an absurd number like 500, no one is going to look at 500 books a month. I mean, not even <u>Evelyn Wood</u>. It would put context around it, wouldn't it? You would go, "Oh, okay, that's 2¢ a book."

Ron: Exactly, the failure to be able to make a comparison could actually make this fail in terms of its message to customers. What's really interesting is by having an artificial limit, nobody's going to tell them in a focus group, "Yeah we'd sign up for this but you need to be more stingy at first." It's not intuitive, and you won't learn that from market research. You have to understand how we humans make decisions, and we do that in terms of context. We compare one thing to another.

Ed: Yes, there you go talking about those human beings again, Ron. We just want numbers, facts, and figures. It's all we want. It's business.

Why Are We In Business?

Ron: I know. There's no room for human emotion, or bias, or prejudice, or whatever. Another thought along the lines of "we just want the numbers," if you ask businesspeople, "Why are you in business?" And I ask this question a lot, a majority of people answer, "To make a profit." But that's not the purpose of a business.

The purpose of a business, Peter Drucker thought, *was to create a customer*. We're saying it's to create value outside of your four walls. Peter Drucker also made another point that ties these two laws together very nicely, which is that the only two functions that matter in any business are marketing and innovation.

It's only marketing and innovation that create results. All the rest are costs. The customer doesn't really care about the costs. It's something he called the marketing concept and I love it because it's simple, but not simplistic.

Ed: Is that the four Ps of marketing, too? Product, Promotion, Place, and Price.

Ron: Well, Peter Drucker didn't come up with those. The marketer E. Jerome McCarthy did.

I love the idea that marketing and innovation are what create results outside of an organization. All the other functions, finance, HR and so on, they're all internal and the customer doesn't really care about any of that. It's kind of what we were illustrating in the last chapter as well when we talked about the difference between seeing the baby and hearing about the labor pains. The customer is interested in the baby.

Ed: Very true. It brings up the whole idea of positioning, too. We have a colleague at VeraSage Institute, Senior Fellow Tim Williams, who has done extensive work on this concept

153

of positioning and how it fits into a company's strategy.

There's a great example from Rory Sutherland who shows a great <u>video</u> about Shreddies, the Canadian cereal that had an enormous increase in sales when they put the Square Shreddies at 45 degrees and called them New Diamond Shreddies.

It was a marketing innovation. They literally did not change the product in the slightest but they had an increase in sales. I'm using literally correctly here, they literally changed the position.

Firms and organizations can change their position in the marketplace, and the perception that outsiders have of them through their marketing message, and thereby create value for the customer just in how they position themselves. This is a really hard thing for a lot of people to get their minds around because you don't see it on an income statement or balance sheet anywhere.

Ron: We always talk about the category mistake that so many business people make about assuming that value only lies in producing tangible things. Things that you can drop on your foot that can hurt you and they down-play or discount the value that happens from marketing, from innovation, or even some of the more intangible ways that businesses create value. Certainly a brand is very intangible.

The Marketing Concept

Ed: Tell us a little bit more about <u>Peter Drucker's marketing concept</u>. How did he come to that?

Ron: This was something he wrote about in the 60s, and it has always just stuck with me because it's so simple, but at the same time it's not simplistic. I always talk about genius being the other side of simple, right? What he said was, "All organizations, not just businesses, all organizations exist to create results outside of themselves."

The result of a school is an educated child. The result of a hospital is a cured patient. The result of a church, a saved soul. Well, what is the result of a business? Hopefully, to delight a customer who comes back, buys more from you, and refers other people to you.

Well, all of those results exist on the outside, and it was actually Peter Drucker who coined the term *profit center*. I believe it was in his first management book, <u>Concept of the Corporation</u>, published in 1946, which was a study of General Motors, where he wrote about this idea of a profit center. In 1997, in an interview, he renounced that and said, "That was one of the biggest mistakes he made in his life," which I found interesting. He said, "Because there's no such thing as a profit center in a business. The only profit center a business has is a customer's check that doesn't bounce."

Ed: Yeah, that's so entirely profound to me. Just by way of a quick example of this I did some work back in the mid 90s for a company called amfAR, the <u>American Foundation for AIDS Research</u>. Talk about somebody that really understood their customers, this is an organization founded by Elizabeth Taylor in the 1980s to combat AIDS and you can imagine that the people who were working there were not doing so for the money. They had a friend, loved one, or significant other who had died of this dreaded disease and we were doing this mundane accounting implementation.

I had an interview with the CFO and when I asked him, "What's the purpose of your business?" He told me, it was, "To go out of business."

How absolutely profound that was to me. Yes, it really spoiled my next question, which was, "How can I help you do that?" But the reality was that we were helping him do that because by installing this mundane accounting system, we were going to be taking hundreds of thousands of dollars out of the administrative budget and where was it going to go? Well, it's going to go to AIDS research.

This whole idea kind of crystallized for me when I met you. I said, "Oh, this also works in profit organizations as well." It's not just the not-for-profits where this exists. It's also in profit organizations where the results are outside the organization.

Profit is an Index of Altruism

Ron: I just want to be clear that we're not arguing against profit. We understand the importance of profit.

But we have a little bit different definition. I think of profit the way Drucker does: *Profit is the price that we pay for tomorrow.* My mentor George Gilder puts it this way: *Profit is an index of altruism.* Which is an interesting way to look at it as well. No doubt about it, profit is important, but it can't be the purpose of your business.

I'll give you another definition that I really love from the person that I believe is the true father of the customer service movement, some 60 or 70 years ago.

Stanley Marcus, who my brother, Ken Baker, discovered long before I did. He was reading Marcus in the 70s and I started reading him in the 90s and I just realized what a profound thinker this gentleman was. He was one of the sons of one of the founders of Neiman Marcus, which opened in Dallas, and Stanley Marcus ran the store during the Great Depression and it never lost money during his tenure.

He took over sometime in the 1930s, and Neiman Marcus sells a lot of high-end items. He talked about marketing and innovation being the main functions of the business and he was very innovative. He did the Christmas catalog, he did the "his and her" gifts. He invented the fashion show, all of these different things and this is what he wrote about profit: "You're not in business to make a profit, but to provide a service so good, people willingly pay you a profit in recognition of what you're doing for them."

His book, *Minding the Store* is simply the best business book on customer service ever written.

Ed: Just to leverage off that, I've recently become a huge fan of the BBC Series Mr. Selfridge, you got to take a look at it. Similar to Marcus, Harry Gordon Selfridge was the one who invented the phrase, "Only X shopping days until Christmas." That's one of his claims to fame in marketing.

Again, this whole idea of value really coming from innovation and marketing, those two words keep coming back to us, over and over again. We have a little model that we've used, *The Five Cs of Value* to try to talk about this and they stand for: *Comprehend, Create, Communicate, Convince, and Capture.*

Why don't you tell us a little bit about the email that you received from one of our listeners about something he experienced.

Ron: I got an email yesterday from Bryce who runs an advertising agency he said, "While justifying a price we quoted yesterday based on the value that we were creating for this customer," the customer responded, "Value should have nothing to do with the price." He didn't want to talk about value.

He didn't want to talk about this idea of value because what would happen? Well, the price would go up. What Bryce was talking about that is really interesting was the fact that he himself was the one who had effectively educated this customer to think like this. As we discussed in the last chapter, businesses constantly use costs to justify price all the time. But it's really a mistake to say that your price is somehow based on your cost. It's based on value to the customer.

It's so important how we communicate value to our customers and in this particular instance, since it's an advertising agency, a professional firm, their frame of value is hourly, right? What is your hourly rate? So, it kind of goes back to the labor pains versus the baby. Focusing on the labor pains, the inside of the business rather than outside of the business where all the value is created, and this is the way this industry has educated its customers. It's what I call ballistic podiatry — a clear example of shooting ourselves in the foot. We have met the enemy and he is us. I told Bryce, "You're going to have to do some work on re-framing your value with your customers."

Your Customers Earn a Profit from You

Ed: Let's go back to this idea of communicating, convincing, and capturing value. Let's take them in order. Let's talk about communicating value.

Ron: If you think about it, value is the one area where both parties have aligned interests. Customers don't care about costs, and want to lower our price, but they want to maximize the value they receive.

Strategically, I'd rather discuss something the customer is trying to maximize rather than minimize.

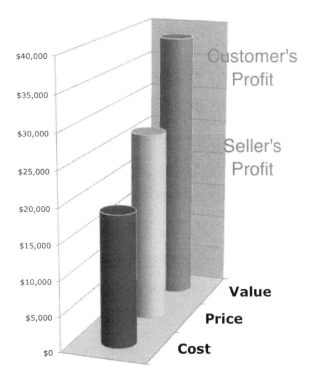

Ed: Right, they don't care about your costs, they always are going to want your price to be lower. Value is the only place where we agree.

Price Discrimination

Ron: Right, that's part of communicating the value and then convincing the customer that they must pay for that value.

One of the best ways to convince the customer of your value is to offer options. We always use the American Express example, the green card, the gold card, and the platinum card. Giving the customer a range of choices, basically, different value/price points makes them decide for themselves what trade-offs they would like to make. That's one of the best ways to convince the customer that they must pay for your value.

Ed: It also creates context by offering options, or what I've begun to prefer to call them is choices. You're creating your own context and as one person who came to one of our seminars said, "Well, it forces me to compete with myself," which is a brilliant way to think about it.

I had someone who about two years ago went through a program I did, where we were talking about offering choices and he sent me an email that said, "I just want to thank you for this idea of offering choices to my customers. When I sent it to this one customer, the guy said to me, 'Thank you so much for giving me these three different choices, my boss wanted me to get three bids and now that you've given me three, I don't have to go elsewhere.'"

Ron: That's one of my favorite stories — talk about an unintended consequence of offering choices.

Ed: Just huge, right? Look, I know that's an outlier. I get it, that's not going to happen on a regular basis, right? But the point is that, as human beings — there we go again, talking about human beings and not facts and figures or numbers — we want context, we want choices, because they helps us make a better decision even if that means sometimes we spend more money than had anticipated in the first place.

Ron: Right. It reminds me of that <u>Wendy's commercial</u> about the old Soviet Union during the Cold War days of why nobody likes to have no choices.

Ed: Oh, right.

Ron: That's one of the best commercials ever made.

Life would be dull without choices. When we fly, we get to

decide whether or not we're going to sit in first-class, business-class, or coach, or what kind of room we're going to get in a hotel, or what type of rental car.

This also proves that there's not *one* optimal price for our product or service. There's a range of optimal prices, and good pricers need to search that range, which is another important component of capturing the value that you're creating for your customer, which is the last of the Five Cs.

Ed: In industries other than professional firms, you're not likely to have the chance to have a one-on-one individual conversation with a perspective customer. What you have to do is you still have to search the optimal price range and what I find fascinating around this in talking about this with all kinds of people across all different sectors is that the light bulb often goes on and they say to me, "Oh, I see where my dry cleaner is doing this to me. I see where the car wash is doing this to me, and Starbucks with Tall, Grande, Venti," and they get really fired up about it because it's true. It's absolutely everywhere once you start to take a look around.

But what about supply and demand? How does that factor in? Because everybody remembers their Econ 101 course where they drew those neat little curves, we have supply and demand, and we had a little x somewhere where the curves crossed and supposedly the optimal price was achieved, the market cleared, and everybody was happy. We cheered and said, "Ah, this was so easy, because we can just break it down to math."

Ron: One economist said we could basically just train a parrot to say "supply and demand" and you have an economist.

Supply and demand is a great theory. No doubt that part of the context that customers are going to compare your offerings to are your competitors, and that's where supply and demand enters the picture.

It's probably a good thing that we're not paying the full price for products and services based on how much we value them. I probably would have paid much more for my eyeglasses, for example. We value a lot of things much, much more and competition is what drives the prices down, or has a tendency to, but that said, the missing gap is to realize that that is just a *tendency*, it's not an iron law, and the other component to supply and demand is this thing called price discrimination.

Ed: Discrimination? We can't have that, Ron.

Ron: Yes I know. I need to qualify this by saying, it's obviously not discrimination based on race, sex, religion, or ethnicity. This was the term that was first used in the 1920s, so this term has been around in economics for a long time. It's called various other things today, like yield management, dynamic pricing, revenue management; call it what you want but I still think of it as price discrimination because that's how I was taught from all these different economists. The point is that this is the holy grail for most businesses when it comes to their pricing function.

One of my favorite examples is book publishers. For instance, what's the cost difference to the publisher between producing a hardcover versus a paperback book? We know the price difference is pretty big. Say, $25 bucks for a hardcover when it first comes out, say, a Harry Potter or John Grisham novel. When it comes out in paperback it might be $10. But what's the cost difference? It's zero. There is no cost difference.

So you have to scratch your head and ask, what's going on here? Well, what's going on is that they realized that different types of book customers exist and what they want to do is get more profit from the people that have to own and read the book as soon as it comes out, the Harry Potter lovers, the people that queue up at stores, and they charge them a higher price.

They still want the business of the people who buy it in paperback a year later, but they charge them a lesser price because they know they're more price sensitive, and it's those types of strategies that you can deploy. Almost any business can deploy these types of strategies, and as you said, they do, if you start looking around. Even Starbucks is price discriminating. Look at its menu.

Ed: Absolutely. The way its menu is laid out, it always put the lowest price first and works up. There's a secret menu item that I order. I happen to be a fan of the cappuccino short because it's a properly made cappuccino and not enough that I can bathe in.

When I order a cappuccino at Starbucks it's always the short, and it's funny because I've tested this. I've got this theory that they really don't want the rest of the world to know about the short, so you know how they call out your drink? They sort of whisper "Cappuccino short for Ed." We're not yelling about it because it's not even on the menu. Again, it's a price discrimination function. But my question to you, Ron, on this relates back to one of the things we opened the chapter with. What about the Kindle? What do you think is going to happen from a pricing perspective on that?

Ron: Well, it's really interesting because as I try to decide whether or not to sign up for that Unlimited Kindle, I'm certainly comparing it to how many Kindle books I buy in a given month and is this a good deal or will I just continue to do what I'm doing, and by not being able to make a comparison isn't this what Spotify did when it came up and said, unlimited music for $9.99 a month.

Ed: It still does.

Ron: I think that's a mistake. I really do. You're right, they need to put some type of artificial limit in there, but maybe they're just trying to get that same appeal to people that "free" is — anything free, we'll grab. Maybe that's their logic?

Ed: Let's talk about how this might relate to other businesses. We've talked about professional firms or anyone who manufactures a product, who has some kind of a service component. It may affect you if you say that we have unlimited whatever, unlimited service calls, unlimited conversations, etc. There might be a challenge with that.

We're not saying that we actually want you to put a type limitation on things like, "Oh, you can only call us once a month or something like that." What we're suggesting is to create an artificial limit that's so high that no one would ever actually get to it, but what it does is allows you to provide context.

Ron: Right. This is an insight from behavioral economics so it's pretty interesting and obviously a lot of the companies are testing it and that's part of what Amazon is doing.

Ed: It's going to be interesting to see how this plays out and of course as I mentioned, as I dug into some of the fine print, your books aren't on the list, Ron.

Ron: I know people don't like to talk about this but the airlines are fantastic at yield management because what are the odds that you've paid the same airfare as the person sitting next to you on any flight today?

The odds are pretty low. It's because they're not pricing the seats. They're pricing the customer, or at least they're trying to. I know you fly with American, I fly with United. They don't come out and interview us every time we buy a ticket. "So, Ed why are you flying to California? Is it business, or are you going to Disneyland?" They have to devise all these little rules about when you buy, are you laying over on a Saturday, etc., but they're still price discriminating. What's interesting about it is they have educated the entire world that this type of pricing is acceptable.

Ed: Absolutely. I can't tell you how many conversations I have had with people who are concerned about if their customers talked to each other and I offer two different prices. Like I sit next to people all the time when I'm flying. I don't walk down the aisle and say, "What did you pay? What did you pay? All right, let's storm the counter. We want a refund."

I mean I'm flying in this tube with them for two hours and we don't compare prices, but in my opinion the reason why that works is because they set the price upfront and I decide yes or no and I'm making a decision. I'm also spending other people's money on an expense account.

There's no reason for me then to have that conversation with the guy who sits next to me, "Hey, what did you pay?"

Ron: Right. If you think about it, after the <u>airlines were deregulated</u> in the late 1970s, if you bought a ticket say, in early 1980, and you found out the person next to you paid 10% of what you did, you would probably be upset with the airlines. Today, who would you be upset with?

Ed: Myself. I should have bought it sooner. I shouldn't have waited.

Ron: They've done a very good job educating their customers. It is illustrative of a point that pricing changes are part of marketing and innovation, which happens on the supply side, not from the customers.

I never got a letter from United Airlines asking me if they could move to yield management pricing. They just did it because it was an innovation on their side.

The Magic of Three: Goldilocks' Pricing

Ron: That leads to an interesting aspect of behavioral economics and how we humans actually make decisions. <u>Goldilocks pricing</u> is offering three options. Three seems to be the optimal number for offering choices, because so many businesses do it: small, medium, large, Starbucks, Tall, Grande, Venti, outside of your example that's not on the menu, it's three choices. Most companies give at least three choices, and it just seems to work.

Ed: Apple, right? Shuffle, Nano, Full ipod. When an iPad comes out it's always three editions. The latest is 16 megabytes, 32, and 64. They just differentiate based on that particular feature, and some others. There is example after example of offering three choices. Just go get your car washed. I can almost guarantee that your car wash will offer you three choices.

Illustration by Andrew Fyfe

Ron: Yes, and the smart ones offer a fourth, kind of like the American Express black card, which includes a detail, right? You'll get a full detail, you might even get five free coupons for your next five washes, but it will be a very high price.

Ed: And some people are put off that there's a limit to the number of optimal choices that can be offered. There is a limit. One of the things I don't like about Southwest Airlines, other than being kind of herded around like cattle, is the fact that when I go to book a flight on Southwest, sometimes it gives me too many choices of fares. I can't figure them out, sometimes there are seven choices for the same flight, which is a little bit bizarre.

Ron: We can actually be paralyzed by too many choices and end up not making any decision whatsoever. Too many choices is a problem, but also two doesn't seem to be enough, and we can talk about that too, we have lots of examples of that.

The Anchoring Effect

Ed: There's a great case study that was done that illustrates our point really well and it happened so long ago that a lot of people are not aware of it.

For the longest time, Wendy's is the old fashion hot and juicy square hamburger and it had the single burger and the double burger on the menu. You walked into the store, I don't want to be a pig, so I'll just get the single burger.

Well, it turns out that the margin on the double burger is significantly higher because in the end it's only another patty. Of course the price is so much higher and the margin goes way up on the double burger.

The solution to the problem was introducing the triple burger, so you kind of walk in, and go, well, I don't want to be a pig, I won't have the triple burger. The double is just fine. To this day, Wendy's doesn't sell a ton of triple burgers. They sell them, don't get me wrong, there are people who want the full on Wendy's experience with the triple burger, but they will never take the triple burger off because the purpose of the triple burger is not to sell triple burgers, but instead it's to sell the double burger.

167

This is what's known as the anchoring effect.

Ron: Exactly. Isn't that a smarter strategy than dropping the price of the double burger to sell more? Just add a triple burger. Not many people will buy it, but it will provide this anchor and it will make the double look that much more palpable.

Ed: Perfect example of why supply and demand completely breaks down in this particular case, right? Because, what we're doing here is we're offering an additional option that really has no relation to the product.

Ron: Exactly. Supply and demand can't account for this acceptable range of prices that we're all wiling to pay, and one of the ways to present that acceptable range is by giving people choices. This is why you'll see a $14,000 handbag in a Prada store.

They don't sell any of them, but it makes that $2,000 handbag seem that much more affordable, and Prada stores that have anchoring items have higher per customer sales than stores that don't have them.

Ed: "Honey, I saved you 12 grand!"

Ron: Exactly. You can bet Prada has tested this. If you have ever been into a three or four star restaurant that has a $10,000 bottle of wine on the wine list, it might not even be in their cellar, but it will make my Far Niente $500 wine that much more palpable and you're more likely to buy that.

That's the anchoring effect, and again this is how we humans make decisions. We're subject to these types of influences on what we're willing to pay for something, which is why it's difficult to know how much to pay for a Unicorn — what do you compare it to?

The Framing Effect

Ron: The other effect from behavioral economics is the <u>framing effect</u> and this is just as powerful.

Ed: It is, and when used in combination with the anchoring effect, it's almost irresistible. Disney is probably the best at putting these two things together, but the framing effect is what do you compare it to outside, like what would be perhaps the next best alternative? The most famous example that is used is Woolite. When a customer is deciding whether or not to pay a premium for Woolite, they are not comparing it to other laundry detergents. They are comparing it to the cost of dry cleaning.

Ron: They even put in a different bottle, where it looks concentrated. It's the exact same thing Red Bull did.

Ed: Brilliant.

Ron: Had Red Bull put itself in a Coke or Pepsi size can, why would you pay $2.50 for this? I'll just buy a Coke.

But put it in a tall skinny can that looks like a concentrated energy drink, it's now in a different category — a different "position," if you will, in the customer's mind. There's a different range of acceptable prices in the consumer's mind now as a result.

Illustration by <u>Andrew Fyfe</u>

Ed: Yes, and these are all around too. Starbucks is famous for this. We pay $4 for a cup of coffee that you can make at home for less than 25¢.

Ron: Right, unless Ed, you have one of those pod coffee machines. There's another example of this framing effect. You're comparing that pod coffee to Starbucks, not the cost of a cup from a can of coffee.

Ed: Yeah, do yourself a favor. Don't take the little lid off of the pod because you'll get really upset because there's hardly any coffee in there, it's mostly empty space.

Ron: And you know who's really good at doing this? Restaurants. There's a whole science, known as menu engineering.

How they put things in context. The words that they use. Do they show a photograph of the meal? Like for instance, it's really interesting, a lot of menus don't have dollar signs.

They don't want to remind you that you're spending money. They take out the dollar signs and they've learned that people will spend more if they don't see dollar signs.

Ed: Yeah, I'm constantly surprised by the higher-end restaurants that I go into that have this 95 or 99 odd-numbered pricing.

When I buy a steak, I'm not thinking, "Oh, I want it for $29.95." As a consumer, I would much rather see 30 with an em dash after it. That makes me feel better about this purchase. It connotes to me, "Oh, this is a good piece of steak."

Ron: With high quality items, the reverse of supply and demand can happen: a lower price will result in less of the item being bought. Look what happened in the New England States this year with the glut of lobster. A lot of restaurants cut their prices because there was this surplus. What happened to lobster sales? They didn't go up, they went down, because people started to question the quality of cheap lobster. It's kind of like buying sushi from a gas station. It's just not the right framing.

The other thing that choices do from the customer's perspective, they change the question they ask themselves from "Should I do business with this company?" to "How should I do business with this company?" And that's a very powerful psychological change that's going on in the mind of the customer.

Ed: Is this manipulation, or is this assistance because you could really look at it as giving assistance to people to buy what they really want to buy, giving them proper context.

When done right it smacks less of manipulation and more about assisting the buyer and making a good choice.

Ron: Right. I don't think you can argue manipulation if the customers keep coming back. We might be able to manipulate them once, maybe twice, but not repeatedly over time.

Ed: Exactly. That's where this crosses the line because it can smack of manipulation. I've talked to some people who get upset with me when I talk about this, "Oh, you're trying to fool people." No, it's just the way our human brains work. When you are presented with three choices, your brain starts to think, "Which one of them should I pick?"

Ron: It's called <u>heuristics</u>, which is a mental shortcut. Heuristics that we all use and we look at three things and we say, "Well, the most expensive one is probably a rip off, or it's really probably more than I need. The cheapest one is probably not that great. So, I'll be safe and pick the middle one." It's a type of default decision. This doesn't apply all the time, but in fact when there are three options, most people pick the middle one.

Ed: Yes, and what's important is that there's lots and lots of evidence that says what your choices are on the low and high end will have an influence as to whether the people will go up or down. So it's really, really interesting.

Ron: We didn't get into this too much Ed, but you start adding a fourth option to the third and you might be able to take advantage of that anchoring effect and drive up sales even more. I often wonder what would happen if Wendy's offered a quadruple cheeseburger?

Supplemental Material

Peter van Westendorp's Price Sensitivity Meter

We simply must get over the false idea that there is *one* optimal price for each customer. There is a *range* of optimal prices, commensurate with the value being created. Dutch economist Peter van Westendorp developed the van Westendorp <u>Price</u>

Sensitivity Meter (PSM) by posing these five questions:

1. At what price would this service be so expensive the customer would not consider buying it?
2. At what price would the service be expensive, but the customer would still buy it?
3. At what price would the service be perceived as inexpensive?
4. At what price does the service become so inexpensive the customer would question its value?
5. What price would be the most acceptable price to pay?

Behavioral Economic Evidence

There is strong empirical evidence — from both the rational and behavioral schools of economics — that offering customers at least three options can often times result in them purchasing more, at a higher price, than merely offering one take-it or leave-it option.

In his book, _Predictably Irrational_, behavioral economist Dan Ariely illustrates the utility of offering options by illustrating _The Economist_ magazine's offerings. First, he presented the following two options to 100 students at MIT's Sloan School of Management:

1. Economist.com subscription $59: One-year subscription to Economist.com, including access to all articles from _The Economist_ since 1997 — 68 students chose this option.
2. Print & web subscriptions $125: One-year subscription to the print edition of _The Economist_ and online access to all articles from _The Economist_ since 1997 — 32 students.

Now compare those results to the actual ad that _The Economist_ offered, which contained _three_ options, not two:

1. Economist.com subscription $59: One-year subscription to Economist.com, including access to

all articles from *The Economist* since 1997 — 16 students chose this option.

2. Print subscription $125: One-year subscription to the print edition of *The Economist* — 0 students.

3. Print & web subscriptions $125: One-year subscription to the print edition of *The Economist* and online access to all articles from *The Economist* since 1997 — 84 students.

Ariely concludes that there is nothing *rational* about this change in choices. The mere presence of an option that was not desired — known as the *decoy* or *dominated* option — affected behavior, leading to a potential 42.8% increase in incremental revenue for *The Economist*.

When two options are presented, the decision is mostly made on *price*. Yet when three options are offered, it becomes a decision based on *value*.

Other Reading

LinkedIn Blog post, <u>The Second Law of Marketing</u>.

Part 4 — The Morality of Markets

Chapter 6: <u>Everyday Ethics: Doing Well and Doing Good</u>

The first concern of ethical reflection is how one's actions affect one's own soul. Ethics itself is a calling; it calls us to change our way of life for the long term. It means grounding ourselves in new habits. It means building — slowly, patiently, deeply — our own character. These are the muscles, ligaments, sinews of the free society. Cut them, and you have paralyzed liberty.
— Michael Novak, <u>*Business as a Calling*</u>

Ed: Ron, would you kill the fat man? That's the question. Let me explain. There's a famous <u>ethics conundrum where a person is standing at a switch for a trolley or a train</u>. The train is going to go straight ahead, and it's going to kill a family of five who happen to be walking along the tracks.

You're standing by the switch and have the ability pull the lever and switch the train so that instead of going straight and killing the family of five that is walking along the tracks, instead, it's going to kill this guy walking on the other track. The majority of people say yes, they would, in fact, pull the lever.

What's interesting, though, is that if the same scenario were the case and there's just a straight track, family of five walking on it and here comes the train, but in this case, you have to push a fat guy onto the tracks to stop the train, would you do it? Most people say, no, they would not, even though in the end it's the same one guy who's dead and you've saved this family of five. That's the conundrum. Would you kill the fat guy, Ron?

Trolleyology

Ron: It's a great question and, as you know, I teach ethics, and we actually use the trolley example, and this is actually called trolleyology. There's a whole book written on this called *Would you Kill the Fat Man?* by a guy named David Edmonds, and he actually lays out 10 different scenarios of this trolley example, but let's just stick with these two examples. There's also a two-part video on YouTube hosted by David Edmonds: Part I and Part II.

When we ask that question among thousands of professionals, a good majority of them will pull the lever to save the family, but then when you ask would you push the fat man, very few people will do that, and something feels different about those two things, doesn't it?

Ed: It sure does. I've always felt, when I've thought about it, there's this mechanical thing in between you, so the fact that you're pulling this lever in a way cuts you off from the humanity of having to touch the other person, and that was really the difference, but that's not always the case, is it?

The Doctrine of Double Effect

Ron: Yes, that is certainly one explanation. It certainly feels different to have to physically touch another human being, and pushing the fat man, it feels that way; but that's one of the scenario changes that Edmonds makes in the book: what if you could pull the lever, open up a drop door on a bridge over the track, and the fat man drops down, so you wouldn't have to push him over the bridge, he would drop out and fall on the track, and people still won't do it.

Philosophers have a very interesting explanation about this. I want to get your opinion on it. It's called the *doctrine of double effect*. It grows out of the just war theory of Saint Augustine and Thomas Aquinas. It says there's a difference between an event that is *foreseen* and an event that is *intended*. In war, collateral damage is certainly foreseen, but it's not intended. If you think about it, if you pull the lever and send the train off on the second spike just to kill the one person, and let's say that one person moves away in time and saves himself, isn't that the best possible outcome?

Ed: For sure.

Ron: That would be great, because then you'd save both sides of the track. You'd save all six people; but in the fat man example, whether you push him off the bridge, or whether you drop the drawbridge and send him down, he *has* to die. You are *intending* for him to die. There is no good scenario there. He has to die to save the family of five. That's what philosophers think is one of the differences. Again, it's called the doctrine of double effect.

Ed: In a way, it's one of the most incredibly powerful words in the English language, and it exists in most other languages, the word "possibility." The idea that in the scenario with the switch where the guy is walking, it is possible, however improbable, that the situation resolves itself so, therefore, that's why our minds will go that way and say, "Yep, okay, it's possible, so let me give that a shot."

Illustration by Andrew Fyfe

Ron: Ed, when I've talked to priests about this, or if you hear a rabbi talk about this trolley example, they say that you have to leave it up to fate, because we are not to play God, so you don't interfere. You don't really know what's going to happen. Yet, I've talked to some Jesuits about it, and they said, "No, they'd pull the lever."

Ed: The Jesuits, you have to understand, are a little different breed, current Pope included. I have personal friends of mine who are Jesuits as well. You never go to a Catholic mass with a Jesuit where they don't invite you up on the altar. They get lonely or something, so I think that's the issue.

Ron: What's your line about the Jesuits?

Ed: The Jesuits were invented to keep the agnostics in the church.

Ron: You know, I know this example is kind of far-fetched, and we can sit here and cogitate about ethics and what would you do in this situation, but we might act very, very differently in the heat of the moment.

Ed: Certainly.

Ron: There's that issue, but I do think it's a useful thought experiment, because it does raise some very interesting issues, especially in today's society how we tend to be utilitarian. We'll say, "Well, look, we're saving five lives here and it only costs one, so, yeah, I'm going to pull the lever," and yet is that really the right thing to do?

Ed: Exactly. It also goes to the whole idea of organ donorship, and the power of the default value. In this ethical case, the default value is where the switch is, the fact that the train or trolley is going straight. That's the default value, and the fact is that should you change that default value, which is what the point of the rabbis are, is no, you don't change fate. Couldn't the same thing be said of organ donorship? By that logic, couldn't we say that, "Well, we should not be organ donors, because that would change fate?"

Ron: Now that's a really good point. Another twist on the trolleyology example is a homeless person walks into a hospital, and the doctor happens to notice that he's a perfect match for five people in the hospital who are going to die unless they get certain organs replaced. Would the doctor be justified in killing the one person to save those five other people in the hospital?

Ed: Wow.

Ron: When people hear it that way, you get repulsed by that question.

Ed: Yeah, a visceral repulsion to it, sure.

Ron: The trolley is one example. Like you said, you're pulling the switch, so you're kind of not involved in anything, but this is really actively involved, and is that what we really want doctors and hospitals to do? So, it brings up those types of issues, but that's just another twist on this; but it does point out the flaws in utilitarian thinking that we can just do everything by the numbers.

Ed: That's the second time you've used this phrase utilitarian. Let's talk a little bit about this. We're really using this trolley example as a springboard for the subject of today's show, which is ethics in business, and we want to make a clear distinction between ethics applied in business as opposed to the idea of business ethics, because as you and I talked in preparation for the show, neither one of us thinks there's such thing as business ethics. There's no qualification. There's no special exemption for business under the topic of ethics to begin with.

Ron: Correct. Like you see on cable TV when they're debating an issue like stem cell research or something, you'll see a "medical ethicist," and I reject that. Ethics is like economics. It's the study of human behavior, and it doesn't matter what sphere that takes place in; whether you work in a bicycle factory, or you're a barber, or you work for the government, ethics is ethics. It's just about human behavior, so we can't draw these pointless distinctions between business ethics, medical ethics, and the like. (See Supplemental Material at the end of this chapter).

That's not to say that certain professions don't have their own set of ethical issues, they certainly do, but it's still about human behavior and, ultimately, we're trying to do the right thing.

Ed: Therefore, what we're talking about here is the application of ethics in business. My simplest and my favorite definition of ethics, just for me personally is: What are you doing when nobody's watching? It's a very Catholic-kind of thing. What about you? What is your favorite way to think about ethics? Is it that as well?

Ron: That's one of them, Ed. Do the right thing even when nobody's watching, because apparently somebody's always watching, right? I have a few favorite definitions, if I may, but one is from a Greek statesman by the name of Plenides. Don't even bother to look him up folks, he's only available on parchment. He actually made the moral case against pedophilia, because in 400 BC, it was legal. It was the will of the people.

He stood up and said, "Is this the right thing?" He tried to make a moral case against it; and he said, "To live a moral life, you must do more than is required and less than is allowed." I love that because to me the law is the minimum. It's the floor that society walks on, and the morals are society's guardrails.

If we behaved ethically only because of laws, because laws deter us, we'd live in a very brutish society, because the law is a lagging indicator. The cop shows up after the murder. So I love the idea that you must do more than is required and less than is allowed. I guess I don't want my tombstone to read, "Here lies Ron Baker. He abided by all the laws." I just don't think that's worthy of man.

The other definition I like is: ethics is obedience to the unenforceable, whereas law is obedience to the enforceable. In other words, our ethical guide shouldn't just be the law. Just because something's legal doesn't make it moral. We could look at slavery. We can look at apartheid. We can look at Nazism. These were all legal, but they were immoral institutions.

My other favorite definition is: morality is doing what's right regardless of what you're told, and obedience is doing what is told regardless of what is right. It's reminiscent of the <u>Nuremberg defense</u>: "I was only following orders."

Ed:　There you go.

Why Study Ethics?

Ron:　Ed, let's talk about why we even need to study ethics. <u>Charles Murray</u> wrote a fascinating book called <u>*Human Accomplishment*</u>, where he studied amazing human accomplishment from 800 BC to 1950, and he basically came up with 14 meta-inventions that really advanced civilization; things like the scientific method, germ theory, Arabic numerals, and so forth.

One of his meta-inventions is ethics. He said we only study ethics because we have to interact with other people. If we were all living on a desert island, we wouldn't need to study ethics, because there'd be nobody to be just to, or nobody to be unjust to. I've always liked that way of thinking about it, because if you think about a modern economy, how many people, strangers, we interact with, it's overwhelming.

Ed:　For sure. I've often said that we're swimming in trust, but we don't see it and, of course, we only call out the bad stuff that happens. Think about this, you and I travel a lot. We go to a foreign city sometimes on a different continent. We show up at a hotel at 2:00 in the morning, and we show them a piece of plastic and they're like, "Yeah, come on in.

No problem. You can stay here a week." Because I have a piece of plastic? Somebody looking at this from a previous century, not even a different planet, but a previous century, would look at this and say, "What is wrong with these people? All he did was show him this card that had his name on it and he said, 'Yeah, come on in and stay at my hotel?' That's insane."

Ron: It is. One economist pointed out that if you roll the clock back about 100,000 years and look at our ancestors who probably moved around in tribes of no more than 50 to 100 people, if they saw a strange tribe coming toward them, their instinct was "fight or flight." It wasn't, "Hey, let's embrace these people or try and sell them something." It was, "Let's get out of here. They're going to kill us or take our things."

Today, like you say, we can be in New York amongst tens of thousands of strangers, even go into a deli at two o'clock in the morning and buy food from the owner who isn't of our religion, maybe not of our ethnicity, maybe has totally different political views, maybe his people have been warring with our people for decades, and yet we buy food and actually consume it with no thought that he's trying to harm us or poison us. Ed, let's put aside the Adam Smith point of how did that bagel get to New York just when you needed it? Because New York City grows nothing.

Ed: Right.

Ron: That's a whole other issue, like the toaster project we talked about in the first chapter; but how do these things get there?

Ed: Yeah, through an incredible amount of cooperation amongst people who never met. That's the whole "I, Pencil" idea as well that we mentioned in Chapter 1. Let's delve into this idea of ethics a little bit more. You teach a course in ethics. Set it up a bit for us. What are some different ethical ways of thinking?

Utilitarianism

Ron: Ethics, the word, is from the Greek word, *ethos*, which means *habit*. Ethics is actually a branch of philosophy that tries to develop normative theories about what behavior, individual behavior, is right or wrong. The four, I call them the Big Four, schools of thought that we will look at are utilitarianism, deontology, virtue ethics — which is what the Greeks, Plato, Socrates, Aristotle was all about — and then, of course, natural rights.

The fun one to start out with like we did with the trolley example is utilitarianism. Utilitarianism was founded by a guy named Jeremy Bentham. There were others like John Stuart Mill, David Hume and others, who also believed in utilitarianism, but the thing that strikes me about utilitarianism is they believe that the battle in life is not between good and evil or between reason and passion, but between *pleasure and pain*.

Bentham was sitting in a coffee house reading a book, and he came across the following line: "The greatest happiness of the greatest number." That was his eureka moment. He ran out of the coffee house and said, "You could build a whole ethical framework around this," because he thought that it's the *consequences* of your actions that should be judged.

He actually developed the idea of the util, which economists have taken and turned into utility, but he thought that a util was either positive or negative, pain or pleasure, and you could sum up the consequences of your actions, and if the pleasure outweighed the pain, then it was an ethical decision that you've made. He actually called this "felicific calculus."

Ed: Good Heavens. Talk about somebody who's just taken it to the extreme and tried to measure everything, holy cow.

Ron: If you look at this guy, he was born in 1748. He lived till about 1832. He was a very interesting guy. He was a polymath. He was a true renaissance man. He was the first guy to wear cotton underwear, and he was the first guy, if I remember correctly, that we know of who jogged on a regular basis because he thought it had salutary health effects. He was quite an eclectic thinker.

The more I study about him, the more I admire his mind, because he was a tremendous thinker. You think to yourself, "What does this dead white guy have to do with anything today?" If you look at the progressive income tax, actually it's more accurate to say graduated income tax, or the death tax, the defenders of that, people like George Soros, or Bill Gates, Sr. — Bill Gates' dad, who is a lawyer — and even Warren Buffet, they will say, Bill Gates, Sr. actually wrote this [I'm paraphrasing]: "If you take a dollar from my son, you're inflicting very little pain; but if you take that same dollar from my son and buy a homeless person a hot meal, then you're creating much more pleasure than the pain you inflicted on my son and, therefore, it's a moral decision." That is the number one argument that we hear for the progressive income tax, and the question is, is it flawed?

Jeremy Bentham Auto-Icon by Michael Reeve - en.Wikipedia.
Licensed under CC BY-SA 3.0 via Wikimedia Commons -
http://commons.wikimedia.org/wiki/
File:Jeremy_Bentham_Auto-Icon.jpg#mediaviewer/
File:Jeremy_Bentham_Auto-Icon.jpg

Ed: The idea of equality of outcome. If it doesn't happen
naturally, we must reinforce it some way. That's really what
they're looking at.

Ron: Right, and they're just looking at the numbers. It goes back
to the example of the hobo walking into the hospital with
the organs. It just seems like utilitarianism can rule out the
individual and put everybody into this mass calculus, and if
the numbers come out right, then we're doing the right

thing, and that's not always the case.

Ed: A full-on utilitarian would say, "Hobo, done?"

Ron: Yeah. I'd love to have dinner with Jeremy Bentham if I could and ask him some of these questions directly, because I can't get a read on how he might answer that particular question. I think he'd have problems with it, but I'm not 100% sure; and, look, there are utilitarians that you can find on college campuses to this day, guys like Peter Singer at Princeton, who say it's quite all right to do an abortion even up to the age of 7 if the kid's not going to have a good quality of life.

Ed: Wow. Give me another example. Do you find that most modern economists are utilitarian? Would that be a fair statement?

Ron: Certainly they lean that way, and I'm not saying utilitarianism is always bad. It's a very useful framework to look at the consequences of your action and see if you're creating more pleasure than pain.

Ed: That's exactly where I was going down with this, let's apply this to the business world. These are things that are very useful business tools. Cost-benefit analysis is certainly a useful business tool, so we're not saying that if you think that utilitarianism is evil because of what it implies based on what we've talked about, that you should never do a cost-benefit analysis. We would be silly to say that.

Ron: Absolutely. In fact, Bentham was kind of the father of the cost-benefit analysis. He just called it pain and pleasure, but we have morphed it in a business setting to cost-benefit. I think where it can kind of go off the rails, Ed, is if you look at the famous Ford example with the Pinto, when they decided not to make the correction, and yet the gas tanks exploded. From a calculation standpoint, they were absolutely correct. How many people is this going to kill?

This is, I think, how a lot of economists make the argument, especially one that we both admire, <u>Steven Landsburg</u>. He actually put out a thought experiment that got a lot of blog comments about if one billion people in the world had a severe migraine headache, would we be justified in killing one person to alleviate the pain of one billion?

You know how he does, he ran through some calculations, and he said, "Yes." You can imagine the comments. "What if it was you, Steve?" "What if it was your daughter?" He said, "Look, you're missing my point. We make these decisions every day about the value of human life." Maybe you're going to go get in your car later after the show and you're going to drive somewhere. My guess is you're not going to do a 75-point inspection and make sure your brakes are safe even though you'll be driving at high speeds in close proximity to other people.

Ed: No, and I love the example that he uses. He says that we could eliminate all traffic fatalities simply by placing a metal spike on the steering wheel pointed directly at the heart of the driver. This will virtually eliminate all traffic fatalities, but it would also make commerce come to an absolute screeching halt, because you wouldn't do more than 2 miles an hour.

Ron: We would think that that is cost prohibitive even though we could save some 35,000 to 40,000 traffic fatalities in this country every year. When people say, Ed, "Oh, if it saves one life, it's worth it." That's nonsense, and it's Landsburg's point: we don't place infinite value on our own life. People skydive, and take others risks all the time.

Ed: It is nonsense.

Ron: We say it, but we don't *act* that way. We never do. We actually do make these calculations. We'll only put a stoplight at an intersection after two people have been killed, while courts of law place a value on human life all the time, as do countries that have socialized medicine.

Ed: That leads to what I call <u>precautionary principle</u> thinking, the idea that you must think of absolutely every possible contingency before you make a decision, because it might harm one person, and you're to be held responsible if it harms that one person. It's really unfair.

Ron: It's crazy, because if you think about the precautionary principle taken to an extreme, then we'd still be sitting in the cave rubbing two rocks together and somebody would be stopping you, trying to argue, "You can't create that. That's fire. That could be dangerous." Also, wealth is one of the best life-saving creations ever, and the precautionary principle can inhibit its creation.

Ed: Absolutely.

Deontology

Ed: There is a story about famous American composer <u>Leonard Bernstein</u>. He live most of his life in New York and his favorite piece of graffitum was "<u>Immanuel Kant; Genghis Khan.</u>"

Ron: I've never heard that. That's great.

Ed: That sets up our next ethical framework, which is this guy, <u>Immanuel Kant</u>. Fascinating dude, Ron.

Ron: He was. He's known as the father of *deontology*, which, again, is another one of these Greek words meaning "duty." Unlike a utilitarian, Kant didn't care about our happiness. He said, "Forget your happiness. Do your duty." He was very big on duty, and he was big on universals, such as no murder, no stealing. He didn't even think it was proper to lie, because he says if we start allowing some lies, even white lies, then the wheels of society will come to a grinding halt because we won't know whom to trust and whom not to, and who's telling the truth and who's not.

Ed: A good example of a Kantian would be Dr. House.

Ron: Yes. I was a huge fan of <u>House, MD</u>, the TV show. It's because every episode was an ethical dilemma, and House, even though his methods were sometimes completely abusive or inhumane sometimes, he always did the right thing by his patient. If you believe a doctor exists to first cause no harm, he did live by that, and he did do his duty despite how sloppy and messy he sometimes was. He always did his duty. [There's a fantastic book on this, <u>*House and Philosophy: Everybody Lies*</u>, for fans of the show].

Ed: There's even a couple of episodes where I guess he's challenged by somebody about unexpurgated truth-telling, then he immediately tells about three or four truths right on the scene that made everybody completely uncomfortable, and they realize, yeah, we don't tell the truth all that often.

Ron: His mantra was, "Everybody lies," (the only variable being when and about what), so he never took anybody's word for it. Like he said, it was a principle. It was a heuristic that served him quite well; but, boy, he would go to the ends of the earth for a patient to save their life. I remember one of his doctors challenging him; he said, "Oh, yeah. I'm trying to save her life. I'm morally bankrupt."

Ed: My other favorite was, "Oh, that's right. We must follow the process. We mustn't let results get in the way."

Ron: That is a great line, which should be engraved on the tombstone of every <u>Six-Sigma black belt</u>. The thing that strikes me about Kant, and I guess it's the most vivid portrayal in my mind, was on the History Channel. It did a documentary on the morning of 9/11 in New York City. It was a compendium of people's home videos, like off their cellphones or video cameras, and they just kind of ran them all together.

There's one scene of a fireman showing up on the scene of the towers after the first one had collapsed, and he's gearing up. He's putting on all of his heavy gear, and he's going to run into the tower and try and help these strangers get out. He glances up at the second tower as it's smoldering, and he says, "That's the stairway to heaven." Like you always say, Ed, "If this building catches on fire, I'll be running out;" but we know there'd be hundreds of people running in. Kant would say "That's his duty. Good for him."

Ed: He was doing his duty.

Ron: He did perish, by the way.

Ed: Yes.

Ron: The thinking is nobody asked him to be a fireman. He knew the dangers signing up just like you do when you enlist in the military. One thing, and I was telling you about this book I just got done reading called, *The Rule of Nobody* by Philip Howard, and he wrote, "The rule of law without human judgment is a tyranny."

Just one quick example of doing the right thing: A lifeguard, I believe it was in Florida, I don't remember exactly; but he actually went out of his zone on the beach and saved a life, and they <u>fired him because he didn't stay within his zone</u>.

Ed: Okay, so the ethical principle of that is the duty to stay in the zone? Or is it the duty to save the life?

Ron: Exactly. The duty is to do the right thing. We had a case down here in the Bay Area where a <u>fireman and a cop stood on a beach and watched a man drown</u> because their life-saving certification had expired and their cards weren't up to date. Actually, a bystander went in and tried to save the person, a complete stranger, and a cop and a fireman, or paramedic, stood on the beach and watched this whole thing and wouldn't go in the water. Kant would be spinning in his grave.

Ed: Right, and I guess the idea was if they had done this, it would've been known that their cards had expired and, therefore, regardless of the result, would've been open to a lawsuit, etc.

Ron: Correct. I know you fly a lot, and I'm sure it's happened to you. You've probably had a medical emergency onboard, and maybe your plane was diverted. It's happened to me maybe five or six times. You know how they always go on and ask "Is there a medical personnel on the plane? A doctor? A nurse?"

Ed: Yes, that's happened to me twice.

Ron: Every time, Ed, somebody volunteers, and I really have to commend them, in such a litigious society as ours, that they are taking a huge risk; but you know what? They're doing the right thing. They're doing their duty.

Ed: Let's talk about this. Let's again try to apply this to the business context. How would you see deontology playing a role in everyday ethics in the workplace? Let's face it, most of the people who are listening to this broadcast are not going to be in a situation where they're going to have to decide whether to save a life or not.

Ron: Right, and you know most ethical dilemmas are not between right and wrong. We already know that difference, and if you don't by now, you're probably beyond hope. You probably knew that as a child, at some point, when your ethical framework was formed. It's actually the dilemmas that are right versus less right that cause some of the ethical conundrums that we face everyday.

Another favorite definition of mine, and I really do love this one, it's from the <u>Josephson Institute</u>, which is a think tank in Southern California, and they say "Ethics is about how we meet the challenge of doing the right thing when that will cost more than we want to pay." They don't just mean a monetary price, they mean sometimes doing the right thing, which is usually the hardest thing to do, will cost you a friendship. It will cost you a job. It will cost you a marriage. It's not just a monetary price.

Ed: That's the application. If you notice a coworker who's figuring out a way to place orders at the end of the month so that his or her numbers won't be hurting and justifying it by saying they're just going to come in early next month anyway. It's things like that, and what do you do in those circumstances? Do you tell? Especially if you're operating in a public company, right?

Ron: Right. I always try and think of the Oscar Wilde line, "No man is rich enough to buy back his past." It's the reputation of a business; or if you're a professional, it's your personal reputation, and you can lose that very, very quick. I'll tell you, if you lose that, you've lost everything, so no amount of short-term gain is worth it.

Ed: My favorite example of that is the Arthur Andersen website. All that's left of the great Arthur Andersen is a static webpage that says Arthur Andersen, and then there's an address for Chicago. It might as well, it doesn't say this, but it might as well say, "Please send all legal correspondence here."

I often wonder what it must have been like for the employees, and maybe there's even some in our audience who were there at Arthur Andersen when the whole Enron scandal began to completely unravel, what it must have been like to go into the office every day thinking I work for a company that has really had a significant and serious ethical breach.

Ron: It must have been very, very painful and, in fact, there was a billboard campaign that Maker's Mark ran at the time in between Enron blowing up and AA being indicted, so it was during that time period where you would pick up the newspaper every day and see 50 more companies fired Arthur Andersen as their auditor, so the firm was already imploding before the indictment, and the Marker's Mark ad showed a picture of a Maker's Mark bottle tipping over, and it read, "Disappears faster than a Big Five accounting firm."

Ed: Ouch. Did you have any friends who survived that, Ron? It really must have been devastating to their psyche.

Ron: It was. I didn't personally, Ed, but my ex-partner, Justin, was an AA alum from Houston, so he knew some of the people involved in the Enron audit. Now most landed in other firms and things like that but, yes, there was an enormous hit and I can imagine it must've been devastating.

The same thing happened to Lockheed in the 1970's. I'm dating myself here, but Lockheed got caught bribing defense officials, I believe it was in the Netherlands, to accept its defense contracts, and it got caught for it and it led to the passage of the Foreign Corrupts Practices Act of 1977 by Congress that forbid this practice.

Lockheed undertook this enormous study. They brought in economists and psychologists and industrial people, and they said, "What makes really smart people — let's face it, we are talking rocket scientists, literally — do these unethical things?"

The report's executive summary basically says there's four things: 1) Pressure to meet organizational goals, objectives, or deadlines; 2) Lack of resources; 3) Peer pressure; and 4) A belief that the decision was in the organization's best interest. I think those exact same things applied to David Duncan, the lead auditor at Arthur Andersen on Enron.

Ed: Don't they apply to everyone in business? The conversations that are held, well this is in the best interest of the shareholders, or the best interest of the firm, or the best interest of whomever. Let's take it out even to politics. It's in the best interest of the nation in the Edward Snowden case.

Ron: Absolutely, and it's even, like you said, more intense pressure to fudge or cheat when you see your peers doing it. When somebody within our social group is doing it, then the temptation to cheat becomes overwhelming.

Rights Theories

Ed: "We hold these truths to be self-evident, that all men are created equal, that they are endowed by their Creator with certain inalienable rights; that among these are life, liberty, and the pursuit of happiness." Thomas Jefferson, of course, Declaration of Independence, July 4, 1776.

What the signers of the Declaration of Independence were talking about was a rights-based theory of ethics. Ron, why don't you introduce us to this concept? This is the third of the great theories, right?

Ron: Yes, and I really like this one, of course, because it basically says that our rights come from our Creator. They're not something that's granted to us by government. The people created the government in this country, and I think that's what we mean by American Exceptionalism. It was the first time in history that we, the people, were telling the government what they could do rather than the other way around.

The thing about rights theories is, there's negative rights and positive rights. Sometimes this is referred to as negative obligations and positive obligations; but if you look at our Constitution, and especially the Bill of Rights, the first 10 amendments to the Constitution, all of our rights are framed negatively.

You have a right to free speech, but that doesn't mean I

have to pay for your radio show. You have a right to privacy, but that doesn't mean I have to buy you venetian blinds; or you have a right to a gun, but that doesn't mean I have to supply you one. In other words, because you have a right it imposes no obligation on anybody else, and hence the negative rights name, and that's how our documents and our entire system has been framed.

Ed: Yes, and unfortunately, the words "negative right" sounds almost like it's a bad thing. "Wait a minute, I have negative rights? That's got to be bad for me." No, it's actually the imposition, the idea that your rights don't impose an obligation on anyone.

Ron: Right, and the way to really bring the contrast into context, is to compare that negative right to a positive right. My favorite example of positive rights is the United Nation's <u>Universal Declaration of Human Rights</u> where apparently, Ed, we all have the right to a certain caloric food intake per day, a roof over our head, adequate clothing, medical care, a job at a living wage, and now even a paid vacation.

Ed: What does that actually mean? If I have a right to caloric intake, I can sit on my bum and wait for people to serve me? Is that what it means?

Ron: That means that somebody has an obligation to provide those calories to you; but what if the doctor thinks you're a jerk and doesn't want to treat you? Or the carpenter doesn't want to build your home? Or the employer doesn't want to hire you? In other words, it puts an obligation on somebody to provide these things, and that's why it's called a positive obligation. When you start thinking about that, start thinking, hmm, that doesn't sound like freedom to me.

Ed: It would be wrong for us not to bring up the idea of Ayn Rand here, who, and this is one of my favorite points of argument with people, although I'm not an objectivist, would be to say by what standard, or by whose standard, are you going to judge this?

Ron: Right, because she argued that there was no such entity as a society, so only individuals could be moral. She does lay out a pretty compelling case for natural rights (see Supplemental Material at the end of this chapter).

Ed: Although I don't see what she sees at the top of the mountain, which is really where we diverge paths.

Virtue Ethics

Ron: Agree. The other school of ethical thought is virtue ethics, and these were the Greeks. The Greeks thought that everything revolved around character. They thought character was destiny, and character and virtue was its own reward. They believed that we were a bundle of virtues and vices, and that the sum total of our virtues and vices developed and formed our character.

If you've ever used that phrase "I can't believe they did that. That's totally out of character for them," that's a very virtue ethics way of looking at things. Is there any doubt that if you are in HR, you would rather hire somebody with good character and weak skills rather than the opposite?

Ed: Yes, and I've always felt that way. It's really about hiring for behaviors rather than particular skills. Skills are relatively easy to educate folks on. I'm going to presuppose some aptitude for skills, obviously. If there are certain skills that people need to acquire, that's far easier to acquire than are they going to be an ethical person?

Self-Interest is Not Selfishness

Ron: Right. I guess to apply this all back to a business setting, business is a serious moral enterprise. You do have to do right by strangers, i.e., customers, and you do have to serve them, and you do have to put their interests before your own.

When I'm sitting on a plane at 11:00 at night flying to some little <u>Podunk</u> city, I'm thinking to myself, this pilot doesn't know me. He doesn't care about me. He may be a different religion, ethnicity, have different political views, or whatever, and yet he's flying me, and he's enabling me to earn a living and, yes, he's doing it out of his own self-interest, but isn't that a good thing, because he's serving me? The fact that money is involved does not make it any less ethical.

Ed: Yes. The good news about pilots, too, is they don't want to die either, which always makes me feel very comfortable, and I'm constantly surprised by people around me who, if we have to pull back in to whatever airport, weather's bad, malfunction, we don't want to risk it, the people who complain. Really?

Ron: It's amazing.

Ed: No, no, I'm okay. This pilot thinks that there might be something wrong with the brakes, yeah, that's okay. Let's get off the plane. Thanks.

Ron: Again, this 100,000-year time span from our ancestors in tribes to today, we have all these strangers out there willing and able to service us and add more value than what we pay them, and I think that's a pretty good way to organize a society.

Ed: Which in our case is this idea of the "soul" of enterprise, which is that business has a moral component. It's got a vocational component. It's a calling. It's about paying it forward. We've talked a lot about that, this idea that it's looking forward.

I know we've mentioned this before, but <u>George Gilder's</u> idea that profit is an index of your altruism, comes to bear really in this whole conversation about ethics, because let's face it, all these four different schools of ethics, we're going to take pieces from them and apply them to our lives; but the reality is that as business people, we have a higher calling to our customers; and it's a good calling. It's a decent calling. It's a moral calling.

If there's anything that you and I are about, it's about bringing that word out to other people, because we just see it persecuted left and right.

Ron: I agree, and I do think business is a serious moral enterprise, and I just wish that people would stop thinking about it as being greedy. Greed has been around forever. It's one of the <u>seven deadly sins</u>. Business has nothing to do with greed. You're not going to succeed in the long-run if you're greedy.

Ed: No, everybody's greedy. Everybody else is greedy. It's always the other guy, never me.

Ron: Greed is a constant, so it doesn't really explain much. To say greed is the cause of events is similar to arguing that gravity causes airplanes to crash. But gravity is a constant, and airplanes defy it all the time. So you can't blame change on a constant.

Supplemental Material

Six Pillars of Character

Dr. <u>Samuel Johnson</u> wrote "There are few ways in which man can be more innocently employed than in getting money," and <u>John Maynard Keynes</u> agreed, stating, "It is better that a man should tyrannize over his bank balance than over his fellow citizens."

No doubt businesses act in a social context, as do all individuals, and should be held accountable for doing the right thing for the right reasons. None of this is inconsistent with the pursuit of profit and meeting human needs and wants. Parents do not raise their children to become rugged individualists, and no company was built by the efforts of a single human being.

Ethical conduct, integrity, trust, and honesty are not just moral principles, they are also major economic factors, and one all businesses and professionals should be judged against and held accountable for.

Character is ethics in action, it is what and who you are. Reputation is what people say you are. Abraham Lincoln likened character to a tree and reputation to its shadow. The Josephson Institute lists Six Pillars of Character:

1. Trustworthiness
2. Respect
3. Responsibility
4. Fairness
5. Caring
6. Citizenship

Are There "Business Ethics"?

It is common today to speak of "medical ethics," "bio ethics," "accounting ethics," and so forth. Yet some thinkers deny there are different ethical theories for these various functions. In his 1981 article in The Public Interest, "What is Business Ethics?", management thinker Peter Drucker challenges the concept of a separate ethics for business:

> If "business ethics" continues to be "casuistry," its speedy
> demise in a cloud of illegitimacy can be confidently
> predicted. Clearly this is the approach "business ethics"
> today is taking. Its very origin is politics rather than in
> ethics. It expresses a belief that the responsibility which
> business and the business executive have, precisely because
> they have social impact, must determine ethics — and this

is a political rather than an ethical imperative.

What difference does it make if a certain act or behavior takes place in a "business," in a "non-profit organization," or outside any organization at all? The answer is clear: None at all.

Clearly, one major element of the peculiar stew that goes by the name of "business ethics" is plain old-fashioned hostility to business and to economic activity altogether — one of the oldest of American traditions and perhaps the only still-potent ingredient in the Puritan heritage. There is no warrant in any ethics to consider one major sphere of activity as having its own ethical problems, let alone its own "ethics." "Business" or "economic activity" may have special political or legal dimensions as in "business and government"..., or as in the antitrust laws. And "business ethics" may be good for politics and good electioneering. But that is all. For ethics deals with the right actions of individuals. And then it surely makes no difference whether the setting is a community hospital, with the actors a nursing supervisor and the "consumer" a patient, or whether the setting is National Universal General Corporation, the actors a quality control manager, and the consumer the buyer of a bicycle.

Altogether, "business ethics" might well be called "ethical chic" rather than ethics — and indeed might be considered more a media event than philosophy or morals.

Natural Rights

In her book _Capitalism: The Unknown Ideal_, Ayn Rand explains natural rights:

"Rights" are a moral concept — the concept that provides a

logical transition from the principles guiding an individual's actions to the principles guiding his relationship with others — the concept that preserves and protects individual morality in a social context — the link between the moral code of a man and the legal code of a society, between ethics and politics. Individual rights are the means of subordinating society to moral law.

Since there is no such entity as "society," since society is only a number of individual men, this meant, in practice, that the rulers of society were exempt from moral law; subject only to traditional rituals, they held total power and exacted blind obedience — on the implicit principle of: "The good is that which is good for society (or for the tribe, the race, the nation), and the ruler's edicts are its voice on earth."

The most profoundly revolutionary achievement of the United States of America was the subordination of society to moral law. All previous systems had regarded man as a sacrificial means to the ends of others, and society as an end in itself. The United States regarded man as an end in himself, and society as a means to the peaceful, orderly, voluntary coexistence of individuals. All previous systems had held that man's life belongs to society, that society can dispose of him in any way it pleases, and that any freedom he enjoys is his only by favor, by the permission of society, which may be revoked at any time. The United States held that man's life is his by right (which means: by moral principle and by his nature), that a right is the property of an individual, that society as such has no rights, and that the only moral purpose of a government is the protection of individual rights.

For Monty Python Fans

<u>An absolutely hysteric and must watch take on Greek vs. German philosophy.</u>

Epilogue: On Purpose

Anybody who's running a business has to figure out the higher calling of that business, its purpose. Purpose is about the difference you're trying to make — in the marketplace, in the world.

— Roy Spence
cofounder and president, GSD&M

Purpose is bigger than tactics. Purpose is bigger than strategy. It is a choice to pursue your destiny — the ultimate destination for yourself and the organization you lead. Purpose is your moral DNA. It's what you believe without having to think.

— Nikos Mourkogiannis
Purpose: The Starting Point of Great Companies, 2006

Everyone has a purpose in life. Perhaps yours is watching television.

— David Letterman

Imagine you had to give a commencement address to a graduating class of students who were about to enter your chosen occupation. What would you say to them? What would be the main message you would want them to walk away with and remember for the rest of their lives? If you have ever had the privilege of being asked, you know this is a daunting challenge. How can you possibly sum up the main lessons you have learned in your years on this planet in a 30-minute speech? We feel exactly the same way about writing the conclusion to this book.

Some would say the purpose of life is happiness. Happiness is not a frivolous or selfish concern, but rather a serious subject, and a noble goal. It is also a uniquely human aim. Aristotle believed the ultimate end of being human was eudaimonia, which is sometimes translated as "happiness," but is perhaps closer to "fulfillment," "flourishing," or "success."

Aristotle associated it with a type of happiness, based on virtuous conduct and philosophic reflection. John Stuart Mill wrote in chapter 2 of his book, Utilitarianism: "It is better to be a human being dissatisfied than a pig satisfied; better to be Socrates dissatisfied than a fool satisfied." But how does one define, or measure, eudaimonia, or happiness? Nobel Prize–winning economist Paul Samuelson tried to do just that in his ubiquitous and famous economics textbooks, where he presented the following equation:

$$\text{Happiness} = \text{Consumption} \div \text{Desire}$$

At first glance, this appears to be crassly materialistic, but it does not have to be viewed that way. It can also describe Buddha-like levels of serenity — reduce your desire to zero and happiness becomes infinite. There now exists an academic discipline committed to understanding happiness, known as "subjective well-being." This new science uses psychology, physiology, and neurological studies. A lot of it is meant to deepen our understanding of human behavior, taking it beyond the economists' assumption of rational man.

We have severe misgivings regarding some of the methods and public policy prescriptions arising from this discipline. Indeed, this entire book is a testament to the salutary effects of creating wealth. After all, to argue that reducing income would increase happiness seems nonsensical. That said, we do believe the question of happiness is important in understanding the motivations of why people work.

It has often been observed that if you define your happiness by your level of success, you can never achieve enough success to make you happy. Studies of lottery winners show the happiness effect wears off after about two years. When one works simply to make money, the work is rarely joyful or meaningful, which is why so many people volunteer at not-for-profit organizations where they feel they are making a significant contribution.

The acid test to determine if you love what you do is to ask yourself: Would you continue to work if you won the lottery? The Chinese philosopher Lin Yutang made this keen observation in his book *The Importance of Living*:

> From my own observation of life, … the great humbugs of life are three: Fame, Wealth and Power. There is a

convenient American word which again combines these three humbugs into the One Great Humbug: Success. But many wise men know that the desire for success, fame and wealth are euphemistic names for the fears of failure, poverty and obscurity, and that these fears dominate our lives.

The relationship between the humbugs Yutang mentions and happiness is indeed tenuous. Witness Hollywood actors who achieve all three and burn out at relatively young ages or seem to live in wealthy misery. We seem to have become richer and less happy. Michael Novak says, "The aftertaste of affluence is boredom." Maybe this is why Andrew Carnegie wrote, "The man who dies rich dies disgraced," arguing that the rich should give away their money before they died. Carnegie worked diligently to achieve his own advice, spending the last 17 years of his life giving away his vast fortune, some $332 million (Rockefeller, by comparison, gave away $175 million).

Even with his Herculean efforts, Carnegie could not give away his money fast enough, for by the time he gave away approximately $180 million, his fortune had grown — through the magic of compound interest — to a sum nearly as large as where he started, which is why he transferred what remained to the largest philanthropic trust ever before known, the Carnegie Corporation. All told, he had given away 90 percent of his fortune, 80 percent going to support the human mind in universities, libraries, institutes, schools, grants and pensions for college teachers, and so forth. Not too bad for someone born quite poor in the town of Dumferline, Scotland, in 1835, whose family immigrated to Pittsburgh, Pennsylvania. Bill Gates and Warren Buffett are destined to follow in the footsteps of Carnegie, each pledging their fortunes to the Bill and Melinda Gates Foundation.

How would this affect your commencement address? Oscar Wilde wrote, "No man is rich enough to buy back his past." All in all, if we were restricted to four key topics in a commencement speech, they would be: vocation, intellectual capital, adventure, and legacy.

Vocation: What Is Calling You?

Business is a demanding vocation, and one is not good at it just by being in it or even by making piles of money. The bottom line of a calling is measured by pain, learning, and grace. Having a good year in financial terms is hard enough; having a good year in fulfilling one's calling means passing tests that are a lot more rewarding. The difference is a little like being drafted into the army and, instead, volunteering for the Green Berets. Doing anything as a calling — especially doing something difficult — is a lot more fulfilling than merely drifting.

— Michael Novak

Business as a Calling: Work and the Examined Life, 1996

Most of us have had career goals. A vocation, however, is something quite different, and is usually not discovered until later in life, after many paths have been followed. Vocation originates from the Latin *vocare*, meaning "to call." It literally calls you to contribute your talent, energy, passion, enthusiasm, and desire to work you love and believe in.

The history of business is the history of dreamers and entrepreneurs, those rare individuals who cast aside the security of a paycheck, mortgage everything they have, and chase a dream that ends up creating our futures. The factories and technologies of tomorrow — that may be nothing more than a glimmer in the eyes of a garage tinkerer — will at some point rise up and supplant the old order, disrupting the status quo and making a mockery of static income distribution tables.

It is the sophomore dropout who starts a software company and creates the world's standard operating system — Microsoft's Bill Gates. It is the perseverant student who charges against the odds despite receiving a "C" on his term paper and launches a company that, most likely, every reader of this book has used, or uses, on a regular basis — Fred Smith's FedEx.

The tempo of business is not one of stability and order, but rather of disequilibrium and instability. Stability exists only in the graveyards. Ralph Waldo Emerson once wrote: "An institution is the lengthened shadow of one man." Mike Vance, former Dean of Disney University, tells this story of Walt Disney's final hours in 1966 in his book, *Think Out of the Box*:

> At Disney studios in Burbank, California, Mike could gaze out of his office window, across Buena Vista Street, to St. Joseph's Hospital where Walt Disney died. The morning he died, Mike was talking on the telephone when he saw the flag being lowered over at the hospital around 8:20 A.M. His death was preceded by an amazing incident that reportedly took place the night before in Walt's hospital room.
>
> A journalist, knowing Walt was seriously ill, persisted in getting an interview with Walt and was frustrated on numerous occasions by the hospital staff. When he finally managed to get into the room, Walt couldn't sit up in bed or talk above a whisper. Walt instructed the reporter to lie down on the bed, next to him, so he could whisper in the reporter's ear. For the next 30 minutes, Walt and the journalist lay side by side as Walt referred to an imaginary map of Walt Disney World on the ceiling above the bed.
>
> Walt pointed out where he planned to place various attractions and buildings. He talked about transportation, hotels, restaurants and many other parts of his vision for a property that wouldn't open to the public for another six years.
>
> We told this reporter's moving experience, relayed through a nurse, to each one of our organizational development (OD) groups ... the story of how a man who lay dying in the hospital whispered in the reporter's ear for 30 minutes

describing his vision for the future and the role he would play in it for generations to come.

This is the way to live — believing so much in your vision that even when you're dying, you whisper it into another person's ear.

Soon after the completion of Walt Disney World, someone said, "Isn't it too bad Walt Disney didn't live to see this?" Vance replied, "He did see it — that's why it's here."

We do not mean to imply that it is only entrepreneurs, or men and women of incredible foresight and tenacity, who should be held up for emulation and education. We will admit a personal bias for entrepreneurs (and entrepreneuses), because we consider them to be more interesting to study than the CEO of an established company. But you can learn from both.

This is also not to imply that an organization is the result of only one person — for it certainly is not. As we have explored throughout, the amount of social and human capital that is required to build a Microsoft, FedEx, and Disney — not to mention have them outlive their founders' lives — is staggering, a feat against all odds. Most of the day-to-day business in our worldwide economy is carried out in the more prosaic fashion of the local barber, and with the skilled precision of the oncologist.

It is also too simplistic to say that all any business of the future needs is an excellent vision statement, or the right type of culture, or adequate leadership. No doubt these are all important, but they are not enough to ensure inspired wealth creation. Business is all about purpose, those internal beliefs and world views that define who we are and what we want to accomplish. When a company has a strong purpose, its people do not have to be "aligned" with a strategy because they already believe in and are inspired — meaning, literally, to breathe in — by what they are accomplishing. This is even more important when it comes to attracting and inspiring knowledge workers, who are more loyal to their profession or occupation than any one employer. They simply can no longer be bribed to do their best work.

A true purpose cannot be compromised, only adhered to or surrendered. The difference between a purpose in a company like Johnson & Johnson and Enron is putting these values in action, even when it costs more than it wants to pay. It is a rare company that survives the ages by putting greed and profits ahead of creating wealth for the customers it is privileged to serve. Money simply is not enough of an inspiration to partake in work that serves a larger purpose, as a visit to any local charity or Salvation Army office should teach us.

In fact, it would be interesting to ask people how many charities they would be willing to work with and compare it to the number of companies they highly regard. No one has pictures of money hanging on their office walls, but rather those things we care most deeply about — family, friends, colleagues, communities, trophies, and memories that acknowledge the achievements in our lives for what we contributed, not what we earned.

Bill O'Brien, former CEO of Hanover Insurance, sums it up well: "The fundamental problem with business is that they're governed by mediocre ideas. Maximizing the return on invested capital is an example of a mediocre idea. Mediocre ideas don't uplift people. They don't give them something they can tell their children about. They don't create much meaning."

Even former Pope John Paul II understood the importance of creating wealth and generating a profit for the owners of the business. In his 1991 encyclical Centesimus Annus ("The Hundredth Year"), Pope John Paul II approves of profit (quite a change from the prior viewpoint of the Catholic church) but also admonishes that profit is not to be considered the sole indicator of the success of the business — capitalism is not a system merely of things, but about the human spirit as well:

> The church acknowledges the legitimate role of profit as an
> indication that a business is functioning well. When a firm
> makes a profit, this means that productive factors have been
> properly employed and corresponding human needs have

been duly satisfied. It is possible for the financial accounts to be in order, and yet for the people — who are the firm's most valuable asset — to be humiliated and their dignity offended. This is morally inadmissible [and] will eventually have negative repercussions on the firm's economic efficiency. The purpose of a business firm is not simply to make a profit, but is to be found in its very existence as a community of persons who in various ways are endeavoring to satisfy their basic needs and who form a particular group at the service of the whole of society. Profit is a regulator of the life of a business, but it is not the only one; other human and moral factors must also be considered, which in the long term are at least equally important for the life of the business.

One trait that separates humans from animals is that humans know they have a past and a future, and they are willing to invest to improve the future, even though they know as mortals they will not be around to enjoy the fruits of those investments. Animals are not wealthy or poor; they are either well fed or hungry. History remembers the builders and creators of wealth, never consumers.

In a sense, there is a free lunch, since each generation is living off the accumulated intellectual capital of its ancestors. Walt Disney was certainly a builder who created and shaped the future by building a purpose-driven company:

> You reach a point where you don't work for money. …
> When I make a profit, I don't squander it or hide it away; I immediately plow it back into a fresh project. I have little respect for money as such; I regard it merely as a medium for financing new ideas. I neither wish nor intend to amass a personal fortune. Money — or, rather the lack of it to carry out my ideas — may worry me, but it does not excite me. Ideas excite me.

I could never convince the financiers that Disneyland was feasible, because dreams offer too little collateral.

The U.S. Marines recently ran a television commercial expressing the difference between a job and a calling, with the voice-over announcing: "We don't accept applications. Only commitments." Airline pilots understand this, recognizing the exits exist for the passengers. Each individual's calling is unique, and certainly passion is no substitute for talent. A higher purpose is measured by the renewed energy it gives us, even when it involves drudgery. There is no greater joy than watching someone engage in their true calling with their entire mind, body, spirit, and soul.

Continuously Develop Your Intellectual Capital

The illiterate of the 21st century will not be those who cannot read and write, but those who cannot learn, unlearn, and relearn.

— Alvin Toffler

One of the central themes of this book is that, as a knowledge worker, your intellectual capital (IC) is what enables you to create wealth for others, and in turn for yourself. Like any other form of capital, however, IC is subject to obsolescence and must be constantly renewed. The most skilled are constant students, willing to look at the world in absolute wonder and think about why things are the way they are. Continuing professional education will be one of the major growth industries in the coming decades, since IC is constantly being developed, making it nearly impossible to keep up with in your area of specialty.

Remember, though, that your IC is more than your human and structural capital. It also consists of your social capital, the relationships that will have a profound impact on the rest of your life. If you think the Pareto Principle is true in a business setting — that is, that relatively few control the majority — think about it in terms of your personal life. Meeting someone and falling in love takes relatively little time but will have a major impact on your future. Or meeting a colleague or mentor who will point you in a totally new direction.

You are whom you associate with. We do not feel the need to

tell you things you already know; suffice it to say, do not pollute your social capital with people who have a zero-sum mentality and believe you can only gain if someone else loses. Develop relationships with a mentor and with individuals you truly admire and respect, whether they are colleagues, authors, or just a friend in whom you can confide. To expand your sphere of IC, become a mentor to a younger person and guide him or her with your accumulated wisdom.

Adventure

We are perishing for want of wonder, not for want of wonders.

— G.K. Chesterton

Profit comes from taking risks since we live in a world of dynamic disequilibrium, where the only equality is in the graveyard, to paraphrase a German proverb. Not content to let the past stand in the way of the future, we all engage in a never-ending cycle of creative destruction. Change is our middle name, and we will continue to embrace and accept it as the progress is represents. We tear down the old order every day, in business, science, literature, art, architecture, cinema, politics, and the law.

George Gilder, writer, economist, and eclectic thinker, wrote of the ultimate conflict in *Wealth and Poverty*:

> In every economy, as Jane Jacobs has said, there is one crucial and definitive conflict. This is not the split between capitalists and workers, technocrats and humanists, government and business, liberals and conservatives, or rich and poor. All these divisions are partial and distorted reflections of the deeper conflict: the struggle between past and future, between the existing configuration of industries and the industries that will someday replace them. It is a conflict between established factories, technologies, formations of capital, and the ventures that may soon make them worthless — ventures that today may not even exist; that today may flicker only as ideas, or tiny companies, or obscure research projects, or fierce but penniless ambitions;

that today are unidentifiable and incalculable from above, but which, in time, in a progressing economy, must rise up if growth is to occur.

Virginia Postrel adds to this observation in her book *The Future and Its Enemies*:

> How we feel about the future tells us who we are as individuals and as a civilization: Do we search for stasis — a regulated, engineered world? Or do we embrace dynamism — a world of constant creation, discovery, and competition? Do we value stability and control, or evolution and learning? ...Do we see technology as an expression of human creativity and the future as inviting? Do we think that progress requires a central blueprint, or do we see it as a decentralized, evolutionary process? Do we consider mistakes permanent disasters, or the correctable by-products of experimentation? Do we crave predictability, or relish surprise? These two poles, stasis and dynamism, increasingly define our political, intellectual, and cultural landscape. The central question of our time is what to do about the future.

Buying — and even reading — a book about change is easier than actually implementing change. If you think of the future as a threat, you will never innovate. In order to try something new, you must stop doing something old. Those who are most complacent and comfortable with the present — or worse, a nostalgic past — are likely to remain trapped inside it forever. It is the uncomfortable and dissatisfied ones who take the risks and ultimately create our future.

A new idea should terrify us, challenging our worldview, the very core of our beliefs. In a business setting, constant experimentation is its salvation. What would you think of a company that had the following characteristics and beliefs?

- No official structure, organization chart, no business plan, or company strategy; no mission statement, long-term budget, fixed CEO or human resources department (don't need a mother and father of everyone in the company); no career plans, job descriptions; no one approves reports or expense accounts, and supervision or monitoring of workers is rare indeed.

- Instead of dictating [our company's] identity, [we] let our employees shape it with their individual efforts, interests, and initiatives.

- On-the-job democracy isn't just a lofty concept, but a better way to do things. ...People are considered adults in their private lives, at the bank, at their children's schools, with family and among friends — so why are they suddenly treated like adolescents at work? Why can't workers be involved in choosing their own leaders? Why shouldn't they manage themselves? Why can't they speak up — challenge, question, share information openly?

- If we have a cardinal strategy that forms the bedrock for all these practices, it may be this: Ask why. Ask it all the time, and always ask it three times in a row.

- We have been known to place ads reading: "We have no opening but apply anyway. Come and talk about what you might do for us, and how we might create a position for you."

- [The company's] *Lost In Space* program, assumes young recruits don't know what they want to do with their lives. So do what you want, move where you want, go where your interests take you. At the end of year, anyone you've worked for can offer you a job.

- Telling people that the company trusts them and then auditing them makes it impossible for them to feel secure. ...We don't require expense accounts because of what they say about character. We've learned that peer control is as effective as reporting and auditing. ...Even in cases of fraud, we shun audits or policing procedures because we feel that responsibility and peer interest are stronger than any internal controls (and that was before the collapse of Arthur Andersen, the king of audits and controls!).

- Most people flourish under freedom, flexibility, and responsibility. Most who have left [the company] have been managers.

- No management works quite like self-management. And working at [the company] means self-managing as much as possible. It isn't nearly as frightening as it sounds. In the end, it's self-interest at work. It requires conceding that managers don't — and can't — know the best way to do everything. People who are motivated by self-interest will find solutions that no one else can envision. They see the world in their own unique way — one that others often overlook.

- The world desperately needs an "Age of Wisdom," and workplaces would be an inspiring place to start. At [the company] we have little to teach and even less to "sell" in a packaged form. We're just a living experiment in eliminating boredom, routine, and exasperating regulations — an exploration of motivation and passion to free workers from corporate oppression. Our goal is helping people tap their 'reservoir of talent' and find equilibrium among love, liberty and work. ...Once people learn to do that ...I know we'll be alright.

After a speech the owner of this company gave, he was asked, "Can you please tell us what planet you're from?" These beliefs defiantly challenge the conventional wisdom of management practices. As individuals whose mission it is to bury the billable hour — a form of cost-plus pricing — and eradicate timesheets from professional knowledge firms, we can attest to how difficult it is to challenge long-held beliefs. But the preceding go much further than these two relatively simply objectives. They force us to challenge nearly everything we think we know about how to properly run an organization. This 50-year old company, by the way, employs 3,000 people in three countries (some of them union members); engages in manufacturing, professional services, and high-tech software; and had revenues of $160 million in 2001 — up from $35 million in 1994. If you had invested $100,000 in this company 20 years ago, it would now be worth almost $6 million.

When we discuss this company in presentations, I am met with a staring ovation of disbelief. As a Persian proverb teaches: "When the heart is willing, it'll find a thousand ways, and when it's unwilling, it'll find a thousand excuses." This visionary leader knew what type of future he wanted for his company, and he was willing to pay the price to achieve it. Is this the type of company — and leadership — you would want one of your children to work for? In the spirit of adventure, we implore you to read the two books by Ricardo Semler (*Maverick* and *The Seven-Day Weekend*) and discover for yourself the possibilities of creating a better future.

Leaving a Legacy

No person was ever honored for what he received. Honor has been the reward for what he gave.

— Calvin Coolidge, 1872–1933

Aristotle devised a "deathbed test," to imagine our last day of life on earth and to consider how we would evaluate ourselves. In The *Seven Habits of Highly Effective People*, Stephen Covey lays out the second habit: "Begin with the End in Mind." He has you imagine being at your own funeral. What would you want people to say about you?

If you study business biographies and autobiographies — which former British Prime Minister Benjamin Disraeli labeled "life without theory — you quickly discover successful cultures have been the result of original thinking. And it is precisely those cultures where original thinking is stimulated and encouraged that leave behind the richest legacies. Think of Walt Disney and the impact he still has on the company he founded, embodied in the continuously asked question: "What would Walt do?" Ben Franklin's epitaph, which he wrote, reads:

B. Franklin, Printer; like the Cover of an old Book, Its Contents torn out, And stript of its lettering and Gilding,

Lies here, Food for Worms. But the Work shall not be wholly lost, For it will, as he believ'd, appear once more, In a new & more perfect Edition, Corrected and amended By the Author.

What do you want your legacy to be? Part of any writer's legacy will be his books, which in Voltaire's words will have provided him "the great consolation in life [of saying] what one thinks." You have read our beliefs, values, and convictions (from the Latin word convictum, "that which is proven or demonstrated"). We have attempted to demonstrate the importance of the shift to a knowledge economy, and throwing off the shackles of the Industrial Era. It challenges the wisdom of the ages because truth is not defined simply by seniority.

We have offered you a testable hypothesis, one that is subject to the falsification principle described by Karl Popper, which is how all scientific knowledge progresses. As writers, we would desire nothing more than having our theories and ideas accepted as part of the conventional wisdom — not to mention next practices — of the knowledge economy. We have stated what we believe to be the truth, and we are now ready to accept the consequences, hoping that what is false will be exposed and that what is true will be admitted.

The thesis of this book has been that wealth is created by intellectual capital, a process of the inexhaustible human mind and spirit. The Mexican author Gabriel Zaid wrote, "Wealth is above all an accumulation of possibilities." These possibilities lie hidden in the womb of the future, waiting to be discovered by human imagination, ingenuity, and creativity, freedom and liberty, manifested in free enterprises dedicated to the service of others. This is *The Soul of Enterprise* mandate. We would not want it any other way.

Made in the USA
San Bernardino, CA
12 April 2015